SON
Salutations

SON
Salutations

By
Melanie Schurr

Copyright © 2004 by Melanie Schurr. All rights reserved. Printed in the United States of America. No part of this book may be used or reproduced in any manner whatsoever without written permission except in the case of brief quotations embodied in critical articles or reviews. For further information, Email: editor@LotusBooks.net
All of the inspirations found throughout this book have originally appeared at www.DailyWisdom.com from 1998-2003.

Scripture quotations may be from KJV, NKJV, or NIV

Lotus Books
LotusBooks.net

Dedication

To God, who is my strength, hope, and reason for living.

To my wonderful husband, Edward, who has been a gift from God. You are as much a part of my writing projects as I am. When others said I couldn't do it, you believed in me.

To my children, Lindsey and Aaron, whom I love unconditionally. Thanks Lindsey, for helping me with the book cover!

To the folks at "The Gospel Communications Network" who first published my devotions so many years ago. Writing for "Daily Wisdom" has been one of the most rewarding experiences. Thank you.

Prelude

" Son Salutations" is a refreshing collection of modern inspirations for readers who strive to grow in their relationship with God so that they may have a more joyous and fulfilled life. A wife and mother for twenty years, writer, Melanie Schurr's devotionals have been appreciated by Church educators and lay people for almost a decade due to their timely and practical applications which address numerous and diverse facets of life such as marriage, parenting, grief, suffering, and improving your general outlook. "Our relationship with God is the most important facet of our life, " states the author. "It affects how we think, feel and behave. However, sometimes, we get so caught up in the duties of daily living that we forget why we are really here: To love God, and one another." "Much of the time, I write from my own life experiences; what I have heard, seen or lived through, and, from what readers share with me about their own life journey. I dare to touch upon issues which can erode the sanctity of home and hearth, as well as our spiritual outlook. Each devotion ends leaving the reader feeling hopeful and appreciative."

Begin the Son Salutation

Before you read, please make yourself relaxed. Make a cup of hot herb tea to set beside you, if you wish, and find a comfortable chair near a sunny window, or grassy knoll amongst nature. Turn off the radio or television, and remove yourself from any distractions. Let the sound of silence embrace you so all that is present is you and God.

Breathe.

Just breath.

Deeply.

With each exhale, imagine any stress and negative feelings flowing out of you. With each inhale, envision clean, fresh and purified air entering your lungs, mind, and entire being.

Close your eyes and feel the warmth of the sun.

Feel the warmth of the SON.

Radiant. All encompassing. All loving and full of rich wisdom.

Greet the Son by being open to His truth, love and wisdom.

Begin reading.

Seeing With The Heart

It's hard to believe I have been married to the same man for nineteen years. In some ways it seems like just yesterday when my husband and I met, and in other ways, it seems like I have known him forever. It is now hard to imagine a life without this man who, like I, have poured our blood, sweat and tears in to our relationship. Of course, along with that sweat, was also found laughs, joys, and deep satisfaction.

Like all earthly relationships, our marriage has had its ups and downs; thankfully, mostly ups, but, during those few low periods when even the sound of his voice irritated me, a much appreciated moment of spiritual rationalism would hit me, and I would realize what was truly important. What was significant was not gray hair or no hair, full belly or abs of steel, but how well we both cared for each other; really CARED for each other. When I say "care," I'm referring to WHO was there to take care of me when I was sick, and hold my hand when I was low? WHO worked two jobs to care for his family because I was home taking care of the children? WHO never uttered a complaint, even when I had gained 20 extra pounds, or dyed my hair a hideous shade of color?

These nineteen years, I have learned much
about love. Not the type of love you
often see on the movie screen where lustful
desires, perfect bodies, and music
fills the air, but REAL love, the type that
necessitates the seeing with by way of
the heart, rather than the eyes.

While today's devotion may appear to be
solely about love in an earthly
relationship, it also concerns the love our
Heavenly Father, God, has toward us.
God does not care about our outer appearance,
but about what is going on inside our hearts;
how well we give and receive love, including
the love He has toward us.

Today, won't you invite love in to your life, by
asking God in to your heart?

Vinegar Or Honey?

"They make their tongues as sharp as a serpent's; the poison of vipers is on their lips." -Psalm 140:3

Did you know that sometimes words can hurt just as much, if not more, than a physical blow to the body? That's right, f or words spoken in anger, frustration, hatred, and jealousy have the capacity to cut deeply. Sometimes, in the heat of the moment, we say something we don't really mean, but once it has left our lips, it is too late, and the damage has been done, unless forgiveness is immediately sought.

We are all guilty of speaking unkindly or thoughtlessly at one time or another,
but the way to make sure these times are few and far between with the goal of not again occurring, is practicing patience and love. Just as a vipers tongue can be so quick it is barely visible to the human eye, we
must practice thinking before we speak, rather than speaking then thinking (and often regretting). In order to do this we need patience; that unseen force which allows us to wait without becoming upset. Then, once in that holding pattern, we have better opportunity to think about what is the best

way to respond to the matter at hand using wisdom, discretion and love, rather than anger or hate.

When I refer to "best way," I am of course referring to the wisest way: God's way.
At the risk of using a worn and perhaps corny expression, I often ask myself, "What what Jesus do?" In conversation with another individual it would then translate to be, "What would Jesus say?"

Not one of us is perfect as we all have sinned in our life time, but this does not mean we still cannot reach for higher levels of godliness even by keeping watch on the purity of our speech. Will our words hold the bitterness of vinegar, or will they be sweetness to our soul?

Today, won't you consider if your words will be like honey or vinegar?

The Blessing Of Friendship

"Two are better than one, because they have a good return for their work: If one falls down, his friend can help him up." -Ecclesiastes 4:9-10

Being a person who values her space and quiet time, there have been times in my life when I have had to remind myself of the joys of friendship. If you are like me, and have moved to a new state, you may find yourself actually having to put yourself in situations where friendships have a greater chance of being sparked, such as in community events, clubs and organizations. Sometimes a friend is right under your nose all along, but you were too busy or unaware to see! That potential friend may now be in the form of a fellow employee, or a nice neighbor.

There are times when it is good to spend time alone with our own thoughts, but time spent with a friend is also profitable, even to our spiritual welfare. Friends can recharge you and help pick you up when you are feeling low, and those friends who share your love of God can also help pull you from temptation or destruction when they are caring enough to encourage you toward righteousness.

A true friend, and the gift of friendship, is a blessing from God. Friendship is in itself, is a form of love, and love in any godly form is a gift from the Lord!

Today, if there is a special friend who has made a positive difference in your life, won't you consider dropping them a note to let them know how special they are, and how much you appreciate their attention and affection? While you are at it, won't you also consider the ultimate friendship, which is a relationship with God!

Heard It Through The Grapevine

"Two are better than one, because they have a good return for their work: If one falls down, his friend can help him up." - Ecclesiastes 4:9-10

I recently received an unexpected email from a woman I went to high school with over twenty years ago. She had seen my name mentioned in the alumni updates of the school newspaper, and thought it might be nice to drop an old (no pun intended) classmate a line. We shared a few emails; talking about life then and now. I was surprised to hear that during her high school years she endured a very difficult situation; living with abusive and alcoholic parents. I told her that my own high school years were not very warmly regarded either, and my own pain was at the hands, or more accurately, the mouths, of some of my own peers. This particular group of girls seemed to relish gossip. Didn't matter if it was true or false; as long as it was juicy, it was worth repeating. While they were wagging their tongues about someone else, it didn't really matter, but once I became their target, it was then I realized how hurtful spreading rumors can be.

♥ SON Salutations

During my Freshman and Sophomore years I was quite naive and shy, thus, I was not the most popular kid in school. I suppose the rumor started when someone noticed I wasn't yet dating, didn't really talk to the boys in the halls, and my best friend, Jean, and I, seemed inseparable. Someone with an overactive imagination decided that I didn't date boys because I didn't like boys, if you get my drift?

During those two years, Jean and I endured so much blatant name-calling and whispers behind our backs that she began to hate school. At the end of Junior year, Jean graduated early. She had her fill.

I began to blossom, both physically and emotionally, in Junior and Senior year, and although I found no boy worthy to date steadily, I began to have guy friends. Much to my chagrin, the rumors did not cease, but the same group of girls decided to move me from one end of the spectrum to the other. In short, they attacked my honor and morals, now saying I liked boys too much! I assume that bit of gossip grew wings after a boy had given me a ride home from my first official high school party. He asked me for a kiss. I declined. He returned to the party. Turns out, wanting to preserve his own reputation as a ladies man, he made our ride home sound more eventful than what it was. I was glad to finally graduate from high school, but the most significant lessons I learned were not those taught by any teacher. I learned to not judge until I found out the facts straight from the horses mouth, and to take every bit of gossip with a grain of salt.

As I grew older, wiser and stronger, I made the decision to not give tale-bearers a forum unless the person they were attacking was also present. Funny how those formerly eager horn-blowers suddenly fell silent!

Now a mother, I have, at times, witnessed my own children and some of their friends, stung on occasion, by the pang of hurtful tale-bearers. Sometimes, I have even had to chastise them for being a part of the gossip. Soon, school will be back in session, and I can only wonder how the young people of our communities will walk in to school, with head held high, or in defense posture to ward off possible verbal blows.

Engaging in conversation with friends is a joy! However, the very nature of gossip and rumor is that it is information which may or may not be true. The rumor may have some shred of truth to it, but with each person it was passed along to, the story took on a whole new meaning, just like that game you play where someone whispers a phrase in your ear, and you have to pass it down the line from person to person. By time the phrase gets down to the last person, it sounds nothing like it originally began!

Be a real friend. If you must say something about another person behind their back then it probably isn't worth repeating.

Spiritual application: Did you know that the words our mouth utters tell a lot about the type of person we are? The true contents of our heart has a funny way of slipping out even when we think no one is listening. However, someone IS watching. God. And it grieves God to know that His children are walking about hurting one another, rather than concerning themselves with what is more important; our own relationship with Him. While we are busy whispering about this or that person who had a secret affair, or the unmarried girl down the street who is pregnant, there are brothers and sisters out in the world who are suffering and thirsty for the attention of a truly caring friend. Our words and actions can be used for great good, or they can be used to cause injury to others. Consider your words wisely.

How Great Is Love

"If you are patient in one moment of anger, you will escape a hundred days of sorrow." -Chinese Proverb

I've been working on a book these few weeks. The book is about gaining peace and joy in life, particularly, marriage, by surrendering to the word and will of God. As I grow older, I better appreciate the simple and quiet things in life, and my ability to smile over these is much easier. I've come to the conclusion that life is, indeed, what we make of it. If we have a shallow and sullen outlook, chances are, our life will reflect this. However, if we seek truth, peace and joy, these too, have a way of displaying them self.

In the most simple things as the scent of freshly mown grass, or a wild flower in bloom, I can find small pleasure. I walk my dog after dinner to a small stream near our house, and when I tire from tossing stones in the water, I sit in the high grass and gaze in amazement at the tiny harmless bugs around me. Upon returning to the safety and comfort of my home, I view the faces of husband and children who, deep inside their hearts, possess genuine love for me.

Upon resting my head in my pillow at night, I know the Lord has me in His care. I have learned to be more content with what I have, and to accept all that God has given me, including the great teacher of life's pains and sufferings. I am now more comfortable in the skin I am in. If others want to sulk and complain, let them. You and I both know that God is good, and life can be sweet if we allow it to be.

As I pondered the concept of surrendering to godliness for a chapter in my first book , a friend sent me the following poem. Its sentiments echoed the words I was trying to place upon paper, and so, I share them with you now. The poem is titled, "Desiderata," and was written by Max Ehrman in 1927, although it has been asserted by some historians that it was found in Old St. Paul's Church, dated 1692.

"Go placidly amid the noise and haste, and remember what peace there may be in silence. As far as possible, without surrender, be on good terms with all persons. Speak your truth quietly and clearly; and listen to others, even the dull and ignorant; they too have their story. Avoid loud and aggressive persons, they are vexations to the spirit. If you compare yourself with others, you may

Become vain and bitter; for always there will be greater as well as lesser persons than yourself. Enjoy your achievements as well as your plans. Keep interested in your own career, however humble; it is a real possession in the changing fortunes of time. Exercise caution in your business affairs, for the world is full of trickery. But let this not blind you to what virtue there is.

Many persons strive for high ideals; and everywhere life is full of heroism. Be yourself. Especially, do not feign affection. Neither be cynical about love; for in the face of all aridity and disenchantment, it is perennial as the grass. Take kindly to counsel of the years, gracefully surrendering the things of youth.

Nurture strength of spirit to shield you in sudden misfortune. But do not distress yourself with imaginings. Many fears are born of fatigue and loneliness. Beyond a wholesome discipline, be gentle with yourself.

You are a child of the universe, no less than the trees and the stars; You have a right to be here, and whether or not it is clear to you, no doubt the universe is unfolding as it should.

Therefore be at peace with God, whatever you conceive Him to be, and whatever your labors and aspirations, in the noisy confusion of life, keep peace with your soul. With all its sham, drudgery and broken dreams, it is still a beautiful world."

As you leave this meditation today, I'd ask you to think about your own vision in life. What type of eyes do YOU see with? Eyes of hope, faith and promise, or eyes of despair and pessimism? God IS good, if only we allow Him to be.

Making Your Mark

I remember when I was much younger and every year our family would go camping. Hiking during the day was always fun, especially for a tom-boy type gal as I was, and I can vividly recall passing many a tree along certain marked paths where people would carve their initials in or profess their love for each other in the form of something like "Jack Loves Sue." Everyone knew it was wrong to deface the trees, but I guess some individuals felt such a strong need to leave their mark in the world that they were willing to risk getting caught by a conservation officer or park ranger.

Most people I know DO want to somehow let the world know that they were here. Some people may accomplish this by doing something wonderful for mankind, as discovering a helpful vaccine, or contributing a great collection of art, while others may draw attention to them self by committing an evil, such as in how Adolf Hitler is now remembered for his attempt to exterminate all the Jews of the world.

Our time here on this earth is so short, isn't it? I know that even as a mother of two teens myself, it seems like just yesterday when I was holding my little ones in my arms as babies. Now, look at them. In a few years, or maybe even sooner, they could be out on their own seeking to make their own mark in the world.

What about you? What type of mark will others remember you for?

It is never too late to turn your life around, and it is never too soon to reach out to God for direction. I have seen in my life, people who, with God's help, break the bondage of addictions to alcohol and drugs. I have known men and women who were involved in sinful relationships, and dangerously affected by negative mindsets, reject evil and cleave to righteousness; all with the assistance of our heavenly Father. Alone we may be weak, but with God, all things are possible.

Begin to make your positive mark today!

He Knows

"O Lord, you have searched me and you know me...You are familiar with all my ways." - Psalm 139:1, 3 (NIV)

Rarely do we sin openly. When an ungodly thought or deed is committed, it is usually done in secret. We may repeat gossip or tell untruths thinking no one will know, and we may deceive our spouse about our whereabouts.

Evil, when it exists, lurks in the shadows and hides in the safety of darkness. Evil does not welcome light and truth for these things expose sin for what it is. Instead, we hide our wrongdoings, thinking that if we don't talk or think about them, they will go away. Sadly, they do not, and our weaknesses find us again and again.

What makes us strong is our dependence on God. This may sound ironic since our modern society teaches that independence is power, but in spiritual matters, leaning on God rather than our own devices allows God to keep us in His merciful grasp. In other words, the best defense in our moments of weakness is to immediately call out to God for where we might be weak, God can be our strength.

It is impossible to hide the reality of our sins from God for our Heavenly Father IS truth. God sees through the darkness of sin for He IS light. We may run from God, but our sins always find us out.

Today, rather than hide from the wrongdoings of our lives, why not consider having a good heart to heart talk with your Creator? God knows our struggles, unmet needs and desires, and He seeks nothing more than to light our way to righteousness.

Learning To Fly

As my own teens near the legal age of independence, I cannot help but think of how, in nature, a mother bird pushes her young offspring out of the nest so that they may learn to fly.

I remember the first time I witnessed that act as a small child. I thought how cruel the mother bird must be for caring so little about her children that she would literally push them out of their comfortable home. While some of the tiny birds fluttered their wings and took off assuredly in the afternoon sky, I recall one little fellow who was so fearful to try out his wings he plummeted to the cold hard earth. He appeared to sustain no serious injury, but for the next hour or so hopped about wildly while squawking in the grass. Oddly, the mother bird did not abandon her child, but watched for predators who could do her little one harm. Seeing his mother was not going to carry him back to the nest, the little bird jumped up and finally took off on his own to search for worms or do whatever it is birds naturally do.

As I grew older, I pondered that same momma bird, realized that the true act of cruelty would be to prevent teaching her offspring for learning how to fly and search for their own food independently. Such an act would cause the bird's starvation and eventual death. As a mother I also try to give my children wings to soar so they will be well-prepared when they enter the world on their own.

Sometimes, like that mother bird, I (or their dad) have the painful task of watching them occasionally stumble and fall, but always rising wiser and stronger.

In like manner, God does not wish to control us, but He gives us wings in the form of a thinking brain and free will. As a loving Father, God desires man to know and love Him, but it is up to us to fly toward Him.

Today, won't you consider stretching your wings and a course toward God?

Enjoying Friends

"Friends are an oasis on life's island." -author unknown

I awoke today to find an email from a friend. Numerous times I began my day in this way, with a cup of coffee in one hand, and my computer mouse in the other, but this morning it really dawned on me how enriching friendships can be to our life.

How nice it is to know that someone thinks enough of you to want to share their thoughts with you. What a good feeling it is to see that another human being is praying for us, and wishing us the best life has to offer.

As the above quote conveys, like an oasis, godly friendship can assist our life by quenching our need for social interaction, which, in essence, is the connecting of two individuals who enjoy and care for each-other. A healthy friendship may also assist by providing the individuals with a support system of sorts, and when one friend is in danger of falling, the other person is there to gently guide him back to safety.

Friends should be a safety net, not a threat. While some relationships can be draining and emotionally or spiritually unhealthy, it is important we chose our friends wisely.

Friendship should be edifying, and allow both individuals to seek higher levels of godliness.

During my numerous years on the Internet, I have had the honor of making several good friends who have made lasting impressions both on my life, and in my spiritual walk. It took time and effort to sift through the weeds in order to find the flowers, but the sweet fragrance of true sisterhood shined through. I use the term "sisterhood" because if a friendship is an honor, and not a displeasure to God, then can not friendship be likened unto the uniting of brothers and sisters who are all members of the family of God? I say, "yes," and this is why I encourage you today to reevaluate relationships in your life, and to ask yourself if they are drawing you nearing or farther from the Lord.

While you are considering that, won't you also ponder the importance of a relationship wit h your Creator?

If we desire healthy associations who we can regard as brothers and sisters, then let us first belong to the same family. The body of Christ.

Depression Cure

Many people suffer from depression. For some individuals, this blanket of dark comes as a feeling of sadness or lowness while others explain it as a sense of doom, and that there is no light at the end of the tunnel.

Feeling down is something every human being has experienced at one time or another, and whether your depression is due to biological or external causes, nobody has to be a victim because there is a remedy!

The cure for depression is hope. A person who feels suicidal does so because he feels there is no escape from his problems. Such a person feels that their burden, whether real or imagined, will not subside, but will continue to worsen, and eventually swallow them up with even greater emotional pain and anguish.

The truth of the matter is, nothing is greater than God, and no problem is too large that our heavenly Father cannot turn it around. Darkness always gives way to light, but in order to see this we must have hope.

Hope is the ability to believe in change. Where God is concerned, hope is ever-present because our Creator is able to do all things.

Where human-kind may struggle or fail, the Lord offers His perfect abilities to those individuals who dare to take a leap of faith towards Him.

If, while you are reading this, you are suffering with depressing emotions, know that tears do not go on forever, for in time they eventually dry up just as every storm gives way to the sunlight. The compassionate hand of the Lord is reaching out toward you; God is ready to soothe your fears and ease your pain.

Do not suffer alone, but have hope that God will dispel the darkness of depression with the light of His truth and love.

Master Of Solutions

"There are no problems, only solutions." -author unknown

Without a doubt, this has been the most difficult few years of my life. A small crisis within our home has pierced our otherwise comfortable existence, and yet, even in the turmoil, light has overcome darkness.

During the onset of our struggle I was angry, frustrated and felt overwhelmed. "Why us, God? Why us?" I would ask, and although my answer did not come as immediately as I would have preferred, the Lord did reply later by showing me truth. This truth was the knowledge that there is no such thing as earthly perfection, and each and every human being will face adversity at some time in their life.

However, God is greater than any problem. Whether it is sickness, disease, relationship struggles or some other hardship, our life journey will never be perfect because perfection is only found in the Divine. Along with the beauty of laughs and smiles will be the sting of painful tears, disappointments and shattered dreams. Relationships may fail and jobs may fall through, yet will we allow these bumps along the path to alter our ability to possess peace, even joy?

The answer, my dear friends, is no!

How we perceive crisis when it occurs can either make or break our peace of mind, as well as affect the outcome of the situation.

As the above quote conveys, nothing is really a problem because there will always be solutions.

The greatest lesson I learned this year is a phrase adopted by Alcoholics Anonymous; "Let go, and let God."

The most successful solution to any problem we may face, no matter how large or small, is to trust in God. As we act to resolve problems, we should never go it alone, but to lay the issue in the hands of the Lord; knowing that where our earthly abilities may be limited, He alone is able to do all things! While man may tell us a situation is hopeless, with God there is always hope!

Write down any issue/s which are weighing heavy on your heart. Can you make a commitment to rest this matter in God's hands, and to yield to any righteous paths He directs you to?

And so, after doing everything possible to resolve my family's personal crisis on our own, I remembered my faith in God, and began to cleave to the Lord in a way that I have never before had to surrender in trust. Daily I pray about the matter, then I hand the matter over to God, knowing that I have done my part, and now it is time for Him to take over.

As hard a period as this has emotionally been, it has ironically also been the richest in wisdom. No longer do I feel overwhelmed by the problem, because I now know that all the worry in the world will not help resolve the matter, and in fact, will only add to my own emotional distress.

Today, I encourage you to hand any problems you may be facing over to the capable arms of the Lord. Feel the peace and freedom which follows the leap of faith, and know that God is the Master of miraculous solutions.

Cyber Dangers

The modern advances of the Internet have transformed how people relate. Some men and women who would never dare strike up a close friendship with a member of the opposite sex, knowing it's possible dangers, may not think twice over sharing daily personal letters with a cyber friend.

While the Internet can be a wonderful research and learning tool, just as we exercise caution in real life, wisdom and discretion should also be applied over the Internet. Like any big city, the Internet contains certain communities which are best avoided. Roam in to these areas, and you may find yourself exposed to words and behaviors which could weaken and tempt your moral character.

Just as you would avoid a high crime area of town, why allow yourself to drift in to areas on the world wide web which could put your spiritual welfare at risk?

The same is true with who we associate with on the Internet. Because we have no way to really know who we are dealing with in the cyber realm, individuals have been known to be deceptive about their age, marital status, physical attributes and motives. We have all heard the stories of husbands and wives who get unhealthily close to an attentive member of the opposite sex, and before you know it they are abandoning their marriage, and emotionally devastating their children as they run off with some stranger from the Internet.

Once again, many of these heartbreaks can be avoided if we would be wise enough to see possible temptation before we enter these danger zones. If you wouldn't tell your life story or marriage problems to a complete stranger off the street, why do it to someone you hardly know on the Internet? If you wouldn't pursue an intimate friendship with someone you are clearly physically or sexually attracted to face to face, then why think there is less threat posed by a similar situation over the world wide web?

Friendship is a beautiful thing, but let us not place the importance of communicating and relating before godly wisdom. If you are involved in a relationship that you could not proudly display before God and your loved ones, won't you consider offering yourself something better than sin? God forgives those who call out to Him in repentance, and this is one relationship you can be proud to hold up before all of mankind!

A Love So Great

A newspaper article tells about how a teenage boy almost lost his life in a near-drowning accident. Apparently, two male friends became over-heated from an unexpected warm spring day where temperatures rose to the mid-eighties, and since the boys were near a large lake, they decided to go for a swim. The water felt refreshing, although it was still very cool from winter. Upon attempting to swim across the massive lake, hypothermia began to hit, and as the boys began to fight the weakness of their muscles, they suddenly realized how serious the situation now was. While the one boy had more meat on his body to keep him in less critical shape, the thinner boy had no protection from the cold water which robbed him of his ability to breathe and swim properly. After a few desperate screams for help, the one teen sunk below the water, only to surface in time to cough up water which had now entered his lungs. As the teen slid back in to what could have easily been a watery grave, as if out of no where, a man reached down and grabbed him, pulling him to shore. Both boys were brought to dry land, although the teen who had swallowed water needed to be transported to a hospital. His lips were blue, skin pale, and body shivering uncontrollably.

♥ SON Salutations

As it turns out, the man who saved the teens just happened to be getting ready to test a new jet ski he bought. He heard the cries for help in the distance and flew immediately to the boys assistance. Had this man not been at the right place at the right time, I have no doubt some poor mother and father would have received the most devastating phone call of their life. That mother would have been me.

You see, the above story is real, and the teen who nearly drowned was my son. The incident happened less than a month ago, and its pain is still very real.

While driving to the emergency room in a frantic state, unsure if our son was living or dead, I realized just how much I love him. Sure, we say we love our kids, but do we fully understand the depth of this love until something life-threatening like this happens? In the blink of an eye, our heart can be torn in two, and a piece of our self lost forever. At that moment, I knew I would easily give my life for my child to live.

Sometimes we need to be reminded about how good God is to us. It wasn't necessary for me to offer my life that day, but as my tears turned to shouts of praise to God for allowing my son to live, I could not help but think about Christ's sacrifice on the cross so that we, too, may truly live. Not only did Christ allow himself to be used as a living sacrifice, but God the Father offered His Son for you and for me.

Such a thought is almost incomprehensible! What a magnificent love God must have to offer mankind such a gift!

Let us not let life and love go unappreciated. Embrace all the beauty life has to offer, and invite God in to your life so that you may know His all-encompassing love.

Life Is What You Make It

Because of a friend who has been going through a difficult emotional period in his life, I've been reading a few psychology books to help me understand what he is going through. I was particularly intrigued at the chapter on how different individuals cope with stress and change.

Certainly, negative life-altering situations are not fully unavoidable to any of us, but how we perceive these circumstances play a significant role in the acceptance of, and success in overcoming the many trials we may face in a life time, be they physical, emotional or spiritual.

We seem to be a people who are quick to focus on the negative rather than the positive. When a door of our life is closed, rather than look hopefully to the new unopened door before us, we continue to offer most of our attention to that already closed door.

Why do we do this? Will staring at it turn back the hands of time?

No. All that we do is torture ourselves with impossible thoughts which only succeed in zapping us of our peace and happiness. This certainly is not our Heavenly Father's will. While it is not a bad thing to ponder the past, even former mistakes, letting the past rob us of our future joy IS.

If there is anything we can learn from this lesson, it is that doors are used for both exiting and entering. Walking in to an unfamiliar and dark room may seem frightening, but by offering our faith, trust and obedience in to the loving hands of God, His goodness will shine the way on our straight path.

Life IS what you make it, and if you want happiness, then seek it. Find it. And, if you want a Divine Guide to lead you to salvation, peace and righteous living, then you must grab hold of our Heavenly Father's outstretched hand.

Get Out Of Your Rut

"Action may not always bring happiness; but there is no happiness without action."
- Benjamin Disraeli

Benny was an average looking, middle-aged man, who lived in an average home in an average neighborhood. He had an average looking wife and average children. Although Benny held no negativity toward his job of ten years with the same company, there was a sense deep inside him that something was missing from his life. Before he met his wife, he thought marriage would bring him the happiness he so desired. When nirvana was not found in that path, Benny decided that perhaps a more noble route to contentment could be found in parenthood.

While having a wife and children brought much joy to Benny, as the children got older and needed him less, Benny felt a bit disillusioned about this seemingly elusive emotional state called happiness. It was not long before Benny subconsciously let go of ever experiencing this gift he so craved. And so, Benny went back to his daily routine, living his average life with his average wife and children, in their average neighborhood.

Benny could easily be you or me. In fact, how many people do YOU know who seem to have it all; steady job, comfortable home, decent spouse and children, yet who are walking about unfulfilled? Perhaps this bland state of existence can be compared to vanilla ice cream. While vanilla is indeed tasty, we must not forget there are a whole lot of other yummy flavors of ice cream in existence as well! However, just as some people are afraid to try a new flavor of ice cream, instead, settling time after time for their comfortable stand-by, even more individuals are fearful of reaching out and grabbing happiness with both hands.

Why are we often hesitant? Most likely, because, as humans, we tend to fear the unknown and unexplored. We also tend to hang on to ruts we have made for ourselves because the thought of aggressive action would mean breaking free of tired and worn familiar habits and patterns.

As the above quote states, there is no guarantee that action will bring happiness, but the only way to find out is by reaching out. This often means, reaching out of our comfort zones and what is familiar.

In our communities, there exist many doors to experiences that could help bring more depth, meaning, and satisfaction to your life. All that is required is the courage to open and walk through that door. Some of these paths of community service and outreach lead to interesting events, fun clubs, hidden talents, new friends, hearty laughs, and warm hugs from people whose lives you truly can make a difference in.

There is no greater gift than love, and in order to give it, we must be willing to climb out of our comfortable ruts and reach out of ourselves.

There is another door we must not hesitate to open, and its path leads to our Creator, God. He is standing your door knocking. Open it, and your life will be forever positively changed.

Rainbows: God's Promise

According to Scripture, rainbows are God's promise to mankind that there will never again be a world-wide flood such as there was in the days of Noah.

"...I do set My Bow in the cloud, and it shall be for a token of a covenant between me and the earth." -Genesis 9:14

In his book, "His Name Is Jesus," author, J. Rambsel relays that when a rainbow is seen from above, it is not seen as the familiar arc of color we know it to be, but as a complete circle. How appropriate this is since the shape of the circle conveys the sentiment of infinity or eternity.

The same is true with the familiar symbol exchanged in the marriages of our western culture, the wedding band. Many eastern peoples also have their own symbols of promise. The circular design of the wedding band represents, not only a clear marking that one is married, but is a symbol of never-ending love.

How brilliant and a thing of wonder the rainbow is! According to Sir Isaac Newton who is regarded as one of the greatest geniuses the world has known, like the spectrum whose source is white light, the rainbow also gives off these seven shades of color. Since the Scriptures often refer to God as "Light," perhaps the colors of the rainbow stem from the pure and radiant white light of our Creator!

When we consider the many colors of the spectrum from a Scriptural perspective, it appears that even in the simple design of the rainbow, each shade may hold deeper meaning.

Blue portrays heaven and infinity.

Red or scarlet depicts blood and redemption.

Orange is for the fruit of atonement.

Indigo was the dark blue dye obtained from the plant; the color of skins used for the Tabernacle covering.

Green stands for new life or resurrection.

Yellow or gold depicts perfection and deity.

Violet or purple is the color of royalty and kingship.

The next time you see a rainbow, consider the silent yet profound message this symbol speaks, not just to mankind, but to you, as a sole individual. The Creator sees you for exactly who you are, and it is important that all people, no matter what their race, creed or color, come to full knowledge of the Divine.

God's word is written all around us, and His truth is just waiting for the soul who thirsts for righteousness. Let His awesome light shine upon you!

Birds Eye View

I love to fly in airplanes! In fact, as I write, I'm seated high in the sky right now! You see, what I enjoy most about traveling by air is the great views you are allowed to see that would otherwise go unnoticed.

From high in the sky, when I look down, buildings that look massive on the ground, appear strangely small. And people? So small you can't even see them! From this view, cities and states seem a stones throw away.

As I peer out my window looking at fluffy white clouds and lakes which seem no bigger than puddles, I ponder life in general. I wonder if this is the same type of vision God wants us to use in times when life seems too hard to handle and troubles seem overwhelming?

Perhaps our Creator wishes we would place at least as much trust in Him as we do when flying, leaving our life rest in the hand of the pilot if only for a few hours?

Up high in the sky, I don't see violence, hatred, pollution, or have to worry about some nit-picking boss breathing down my neck. I am free to simply sit back, relax, enjoy the view and leave the driving to someone else. If only we could trust God and live life with this same type of innocence.

If you are facing some sort of difficulty in your life, and troubles seem to overwhelm you, close your eyes, think of flight, and how faith in God gives you the wings to overcome adversity. Hardships which seem large today, will soon be nothing more than a thought of the past, so set your sights on God and let Him set your course.

Singing The Blues

At one time or another we all have periods of sadness in life. However, anyone who has experienced full-blown depression, otherwise known as "the blues," will tell you there is a huge difference between the two emotions. When a person feels a little low or sad, there is usually the realization that a light exists at the end of the tunnel. However, clinical depression can be so severe that there is often a sense of hopelessness, and that there is no way out from the darkness.

According to Miriam Rosenthal, M.D., one out of six adults have experienced symptoms of depression. The illness knows no difference between race, age or religious background, and about 25% of all women have experienced it, and 12% of all men.

Many people think you can just tell a depressed person to "just snap out of it," but the reality of depression is that its roots often reach deeper, and there are often very real physical, (medical), problems which underlay it. Some women are even known to have "Post Partum Depression," which can occur after a female delivers a baby. Another cause of depression can be "Bipolar Disorder," which is caused by a chemical imbalance within the body.

Prolonged periods of sadness can turn in to serious depression because repeated emotional blows have the ability to break down our coping mechanisms. The end result can be overwhelming feelings of anxiety, guilt, worthlessness, helplessness, inability to concentrate or make decisions, and decreased energy.

If any of these describe what you might be feeling, there are steps you can be taking so that the light at the end of the tunnel is clearly visible. These include:

See a Dr. and have a complete physical. Talk to a professional counselor. Eat a well-balanced diet. Exercise daily. Lean on God.

This last recommendation may surprise you, but what better Being to cast our troubles and cares to, but our Creator? Even when we may think our thoughts and actions are secret, nothing is hidden from the Lord. Not only does God know our joys, but He feels our pains, and is just waiting for us to reach out so that He may dry our tears.

Won't you call on your Creator today?

Feeling Persecuted?

"Blessed are you when people insult you, persecute you and falsely say all kinds of evil against you because of me. Rejoice and be glad, because great is your reward in heaven, for in the same way they persecuted the prophets who were before you." -Matthew 5:11,12 NIV

Have you ever felt a little picked on? Maybe some kids at school are harassing you because they don't like your clothing choices or hair style? Or maybe the persecution you feel is a result of employees at work who are taking you for granted, piling more papers upon your desk when you are already swamped?

If you are the parent of a teen, maybe you are going through a very hard time dealing with your child's puberty hormones which can cause him to be unpredictably moody?

Dark and heavy days are something we all encounter now and then. During such periods, it's easy to feel like the weight of the world is upon your shoulders, and that just about everyone is against you, or simply does not understand. In some cases there is real persecution going on, and in other instances, mood, hormones or stress simply causes you to feel attacked.

Whatever the case may be, we must accept the fact that just as sun rises, so too, will the rain fall. In other words, although the sky may seem dark and dreary now, in due time light makes its presence known.

There will be times we are picked on for what we believe in, or for doing the right thing, but rest assured, even the Son of God endured mockery and persecution for righteousness sake.

Today, if you are feel like your load is too heavy to bear, hand in over to the Lord, and He will be swift to carry your burdens for you. Remember, He too, has shed tears and knows the sting of suffering, and those who cast their cares to the Lord will be rewarded with salvation.

Circle Of Love

The term "inner circle" is used to define those people who are most important in your life, be they solely your immediate family, friends and close relations, or some other personal grouping. These are the relationships you tend to invest the most time and energy in to, thus, their effect on our emotional state is more profound than, say, how we might react when communicating with someone who is outside of this circle. For example, if, while walking down a busy sidewalk in the heart of New York City, a man you have never seen before glares at you and growls, "I hate you," chances are good you will not be adversely affected, but you will roll your eyes, brush off the comment thinking the man is in need of a mental health professional, and continue on about your merry way. However, have someone who is in your inner circle mutter this same negative statement, and most individuals will react strongly, the words acting as tiny daggers to our heart.

Consider the constantly meddling and berating mother-in-law, and the effect such continual attacks may have on her adult child and their family. Or, what about the parent who puts down his teen whenever he is angry with him?

Just as the cylindrical shape of the wedding band symbolizes the never-ending circle of love in marriage, the proverbial "inner circle" representing those relationships most dear to us should be regarded as equally precious. Both are deserving of respect, care and the utmost attention so that the circle of love is not weakened or hindered by thoughtless words or actions.

There is another circle of love which exists, but sadly, some people will never experience its manifold blessings. The circle is the never-ceasing love between God and man; a continual bond which links us with the Divine. Its reward is eternal life and salvation, and it is freely placed upon the heart of any man who humbly calls upon the name of the Lord.

Worth Fighting For

One of my kids recently said to me, "Mom, you like causing trouble!" Knowing such was not the case, I was just about ready to take the comment in a derogatory manner when the truth of what he was really trying to say occurred to me. "Well, actually, " I said, as I grinned knowingly, "I think a more accurate statement is that I am not afraid to fight when need be."

Just as there are times to laugh, and other times to cry, so too are there circumstances in life when we must decide if something is important enough to fight for. Right off the bat, I can think of one great reason; my children.

Just as a gentle mother bear will turn instantly aggressive if a stranger threatens to harm her cubs, so too is it sometimes necessary for a parent to protect his or her own children. Like an old-time movie, my mind momentarily reflects back when neighborhood bullies were harassing my then, five year old daughter. Boys may be boys, but threaten to do harm to my kid, and you'll find your self being chased down the street by one scowling mom!

Marriage is another medium I am willing to

work and fight for. Talk to couples who have been married for twenty to fifty years, and they will attest to the fact long-lasting good marriages are not continual daily bliss, but are exactly as our wedding vows state, "through sickness and in health, good times and bad." If we run at the slightest wind of change, and don't fight for love when it is challenged and pushed to its limits, then love is not as durable as we are told it is.

Thankfully, it is!

Within our own historical roots, we, American's, have also had to fight f or our freedom, and to defend our great nation. No one prefers to engage in battle, but if we realistically consider the alternative, sometimes, strong statements need to be made. I am willing to fight for my hopes and my dreams so that I can turn visions in to realities.

I am willing to defend my beliefs, and fight for what I believe is truth and justice.

If there is anything I can teach my children, it is to not be afraid to stand up for what is important. Be willing to have a little mud slung your way when you do, and if you get a

♥ SON Salutations

little dirt under your nails, so what? And, if you need inspiration, just look to Christ Jesus who endured mockery, betrayal, suffering, even, death, in order to bring to you and I the greatest gift known to man; from love sprung the gift of eternal life.

Better to be dirty than dead.

Birds Of A Feather

I recently had to give a lecture to my son. It was a difficult subject to approach since he is at that stage where he would prefer to make his own choices rather than have mom or dad offer their wisdom and experience. The topic was choosing friends. Being somewhat of a free-spirit myself who appreciates uniqueness and diversity, I often enjoy people who march to the beat of a different drummer. However, when a chosen path leads to some sort of ungodliness, that is where wisdom and discretion need to reign supreme. For example, if you are a recovering alcoholic, do you chose friends who go nightly bar-hopping, also inviting you to join them? Sure, you may swear you won't touch a drop of liquor, but the temptation is far greater in that type of environment than it would be in a place where no alcohol was served.

I knew a man in such a situation, and while he fought the urge for weeks, it was not long before one innocent drink with his friends lead to many more nights of fall-down drunkenness. One morning, when he awoke in a hospital with a concussion, a hangover, and word of his now demolished car, he knew it was time to chose a new set of best friends.

Many months later he told me that he finally came to clearly see that the only bond he and these buddies shared was the alcohol, so while it initially panged him to break a tie which he perceived as important, truth and time quickly healed that hurt.

What about you? Do the people you associate with encourage you toward godliness or evil?

Real friends do not wish to see you hurt in mind, body or spirit.

God is our heavenly Father, but He is also friend who desires our utmost blessings in life. He does not joy during our times of despair, but offer His hand of comfort for those who call on Him.

Giving up a relationship due to its ungodliness may be difficult, but rejecting your salvation has even more dire consequences.

Material vs. Spiritual

"'The silver is mine and the gold is mine,' declares the Lord Almighty." - Haggai 2:8 (NIV)

Isn't it ironic that man works so ardently to own his own home, shiny car, and adorn our fingers with precious gems, and try as hard as we may, what we so-called "own" is not really ours anyway!

"What?" you say, "How can that be?"

Here is the scoop.

Everything which God created, from the silver, diamonds, furs and gold, our Heavenly Father owns. For that matter, we owe our very life, not just to our parents, but to the Savior Himself, for without His divine intervention mankind would not even exist. You see, you and I are not on this planet to make a name for ourselves in the business world, or to gather all the material items we can afford, nor even to eat, drink and be merry. Certainly, God wishes our ultimate joy and happiness, but our greater purpose is to worship God and love one another.

Again you say, "What? How can I worship God when I can't even see Him?"

♥ SON Salutations

Everything we do and say is a testament to our faith in God - or lack thereof. Either our deeds will glorify Him, or bring Him shame.

"Yes, but is it realistic to expect us to also love one another," you then say, "I mean, are we to also love those who murder, steal and rob us of our freedom?"

Love can take many shapes and forms. Certainly, love can be warm and mushy, and consist of hugs, kisses and kind words, but love also stands for truth and justice. The truth CAN be spoken in love, and although truth may sometimes sting, that pang may save someone's soul.

The next time you are thinking about keeping up with the Joneses, and worrying about how to get your next raise so you can buy that great vacation home in Hawaii, think of this little story and then ask, "What can I do to better glorify God?"

The "Giving" Drink

Being the sometimes adventurous health-conscious individual I am, upon hearing about an increasingly popular home-brewed unique tea which has a reputation for being beneficial to your health, I decided to give it a try. Brewing it would not be easy though, or unlike most store-bought teas you can simply purchase at the local grocery store, this drink, known as "Kombucha," must be passed on from a friend. Let me explain.

Kombucha is a beverage which is typically made by fermenting common black tea and white sugar using a special Kombucha colony. It is this active culture which is first needed before you can brew the tasty drink which some people compare to tart apple cider. The culture, however, may only be obtained and utilized while it is live, and since each time a batch of Kombucha tea is prepared it produces a new culture, you must first find someone who is willing to share their new culture so that you can then make your own tea.

My ardent search for such a person took me to a popular auction web site on the Internet, but after the deal fell through, and I lost my money AND the Kombucha culture, I became discouraged, not knowing where else to turn.

♥ SON Salutations

Then I met "Marjorie."

I found Marjorie's contact information from a site on the Internet which basically hooks up private Kombucha sellers with individual buyers. What intrigued me about Marjorie's ad was that it stated she offered Kombucha cultures for free! In fact, several of the sellers made note that they were so blessed by the acclaimed health benefits of the exotic drink, giving away an active Kombucha culture to someone who needed one was their way of giving back to society.

Sorry to say, I was somewhat suspicious, thinking that there must be some sort of catch as no one gives something for nothing these days. "The clincher must be in the shipping and handling," I thought. "They probably offer the product for free and then double up on the shipping expense!" That theory was blown to bits when Marjorie wrote me back saying there was no added or hidden costs, and any shipping charge would come out of her own pocket.

Now I was really baffled! Yes, I am a Christian who knows Christ taught us about the beauty of giving and receiving with a cheerful heart, but it had been such a long time since anyone had blessed me in this way that I suppose I had forgotten that there are still many good people in the world. Again Marjorie wrote, telling me not to worry, that everything I would need to brew my first batch of Kombucha would also be included in the package.

No longer suspicious, but still in awe, I wrote Marjorie back to find out more about her gracious spirit of generosity towards a complete stranger. With her permission, this is what she wrote:

"My husband and I have been blessed with many things and it's my way of giving back to people. We are not rich but I share what I do have. If I cannot afford it then I will ask for postage, but for now, it's my way of giving. It's just what I do. I guess you would call it a spiritual reason. My friend gave me my first one for nothing and shared graciously so I will do the same as long as I can. If I have as many requests in the future as I did this week I would be unable, but for now it's ok. Others that I could not repay have blessed me in my times of need so when I can do for others, I do it. You never know when a blessing will come back to you! When you give your first baby (Kambucha culture) away you will know the joy!"

I don't know how to explain it, but Marjorie's good deed was as a bright ray of sunshine which rekindled what may have been my admittedly waning trust in mankind.

How easy it is for us to begin to feel skeptical and cynical, especially when we hear so many reports of war, violence, and the declining morality of man on television and in the newspaper. Yet, as this kind gesture shows, God is still in control, and goodness still reigns supreme. We may need to be reminded now and then, and that is when God can and does work through the works and words of His children.

The story does not end there for it is in this same spirit of giving that God gave to mankind His Son so that we may have life more abundantly. He gave to us the ability to call out to the Divine; for forgiveness, comfort, praise and salvation. His gifts are free, and the only price to pay is the simple peace and joy making Him a part of your life will offer your heart.

Fake Diamonds

Consider for a moment if you will, the similarities between a diamond and the fake stone known as cubic zirconium. Both possess a certain clarity and sparkle, yet one is considered precious, while the other falls into the category of cheap jewelry.

In similar manner, sometimes sin can appear very appealing, yet when more closely examined, the foundation of sin is evil, and its path leads to destruction. This is how Satan works. He masks evil to make it appeal to man's senses. Our flesh may tingle and find pleasure for a time while flirting with sin, but just when you think your sins will never find you out, it does, and this is when heartbreak begins, families are often devastated, and marriages begin to crumble. Of course, there is also the personal price we pay spiritually.

Just as you would not purchase a beautiful diamond haphazardly, we should not take our spiritual welfare for granted. Test and try all things to see if they are from God or Satan; fleeing from evil, and cleaving to goodness.

Seek God, and do not be mislead by cheap imitations.

Maiden Names

When I first married almost twenty years ago, not only did I feel excited at the idea of having a husband and children, but at the same time, I felt like I was losing a part of myself; my identity. I am of course referring to how a woman, upon her wedding day, releases her maiden name, then takes on the name of her husband. Forever gone is the identity she always knew, and there is a combination of sadness and joy; excitement over a new beginning!

After so many years of marriage, my spouse's name is now a part of who I am. I have come to embrace this name for it represents not who I was, but who I now am as a mature woman who is both wife and mother.

It is amazing how, in the blink of an eye, a soon-to-be wedded female can change from one name to another.

I cannot help but be reminded of how the Lord can also transform lives, cleansing the hearts of those who sincerely call upon Him in repentance. At this moment, our slate is washed clean of past repented of sins, and a new beginning is ours for the taking! No longer are we the same, but we are transformed; new creations in Christ Jesus!

Just as marriage provides us with a fresh start, a new phase in life, so too, does God offer you an even greater gift; eternal salvation! As does the husband and wife wear a wedding band upon their fingers, the Lord's name is engraved upon the hearts of those who believe in Him. No longer do we look back to the hurtful past which previously was sinful, but we are called to start anew and look to the hope of a righteous present and future!

A husband is a wonderful life-partner, indeed, but an intimate relationship with God is even greater!

In Search of Perfection

"Everything has its wonders, even darkness and silence, and I learn, whatever state I may be in, therein to be content." - Helen Keller

It has occurred to me that we are sometimes a very spoiled people. Certainly, we are to be grateful we live in a world with numerous modern advances, but have we come to expect too much? I am referring to the search for perfection.

We read fashion magazines and see models on the run-way, and we feel disappointment when our own bodies do not match up. We meet new acquaintances at a social gathering, and when we find out they have educational degrees we may not possess, thoughts of inferiority overwhelm us.

The same is true with artistic depictions of the perfect Thanksgiving or Christmas, such as those created by Norman Rockwell. We ponder our own families and they seem so dysfunctional.

How ironic that a deaf and blind woman who faced much adversity in her life can teach us that, even in life's bumps and bruises, there is something to be gained. What Helen Keller learned was that if the hills and valleys cannot always be avoided, it is wise to look for the wisdom each of these circumstances may offer. For example, Miss Keller lacked the ability to hear and see, yet despite what some people may call flaws, Helen Keller had a very sophisticated intelligence which allowed her to ponder and reveal profound thoughts. Lacks allowed this woman to be strong in other ways.

In my own life I have encountered some adversity, yet, when I reflect back, I now see what a great teacher life has been. Some of my greatest wisdom has come through pain, struggle and adversity.

When we seek a perfect world, perfect bodies, perfect brains and perfect relationships, we prevent happiness from reaching us because we compare our own flawed, imperfect and error-ridden lives to an impossible societal standard.

As did Miss Keller accept life's inevitable hardships; making the best out of all things, so too, does God not desire man to seek earthly perfection, but spiritual perfection. Please God, not man.

Blessed

Isn't it interesting that many people tend to focus on what they don't have rather than on what is good in their life?

Think about it. While we are frustrated over not being able to find that perfect outfit in our closet, there is someone out in the world who is thankful they at least have one article of clothing to keep them warm. As we peer out the window of our home, jealous we do not possess the larger home of our neighbor, some human being is thankful he at least has a large box or the underside of a bridge to keep him safe from the elements.

While we complain to the waiter our steak is too well-done, or our shrimp is a little cold, a small child is thankful he at least has a glass of clean water and stale bread scraps to eat.

Sadly, we often tend to treat our loved-ones the same way, focusing on their lacks and flaws, rather than enjoying their strengths and admirable qualities. In the end, it is we who suffer most because of our own distorted mind-set.

Today, I challenge you to wake up with a new vision, eyes that drink in the beauty and goodness of life, rather than filter happiness out. This new sight is easily obtainable by calling out to God. You see, God is truth and love, and if it is the purity of righteousness we seek, this is freely given to those who know God.

Water Your Own Garden

It has occurred to me that many spouses do not water their garden adequately. "What is she talking about," you say, "I don't even have a garden!"

You may not have a garden in the traditional sense, but do you know your marriage can be likened unto a garden as well?

Within the institution of marriage is a sacred foundation which should be carefully nurtured so that it may beautifully thrive. Within this proverbial small plot of land, we must till the soil so plants may breathe and spread their roots, yanking out weeds which may choke them and prevent the seedlings from growing. Within this same godly terrain, it is often necessary to built up a small fence around the garden, to prevent hungry animals from stealing what we have carefully planted and nurtured. Lastly, every garden needs plenty of water and sunshine, but the radiance I speak of now, refers to that which comes from the Son, not the sun.

As the most attentive gardener, a truly thriving marriage needs the loving care of God and His Son, Jesus Christ, to bless and protect this institution from all forms of ungodliness.

As I previously stated, many people who find themselves in a less than fulfilling marriage, stand where they are because the two caretakers of the garden did not realize how important it is to constantly care for their sacred terrain. Every husband or wife is guilty of this at one time or another, including myself, and it is especially easy to neglect those things which are not clearly visible, yet are the very foundation of a successful marriage. Fail to water things such as love, honor, and respect, and the very roots of marriage begin to weaken. Ignore such things as small un-addressed hurts, and leaves begin to wither. Ration much needed water, and the once fertile soil of marriage begins to dehydrate. Water someone else's garden and not your own, and watch your garden quickly
turn in to a barren desert where thorns and thickets now replace beautiful blooms. Cross-contamination also quickly spreads because a garden sprinkled with polluted waters is just as deadly as failing to water at all.

I've spoken to many discontented spouses, hearing such comments as, "She doesn't care about my needs," "He doesn't listen anymore," "What happened to the romance?"

Each one of these concerns is a seed which has the potential of becoming a flower or a weed. What determines the future of each seed is if we will take the time, energy and care to dig down deep in the soil, and to offer each seed the gift of ourselves.

Are there un-addressed issues? Then address them! Are their hurts and neglects? Then feed and heal them!

Just as it is wise to water our own gardens, we must also regard our relationship with God just as tenderly; taking care to water our faith with the word of God, and pulling out weeds which may threaten our walk.

How does YOUR garden grow?

Renewed Interest

It's amazing how a seemingly meaningless idea or sight can re-ignite enthusiasm for something for which we once had a strong passion. For example, I know many long-term married couples who, at various points in their marriage, fall in a rut of complacency. After a while, some small yet profound epiphany will set them on the right track, thus correcting the former act of taking each other for granted.

Recently, I stumbled upon the site of a well-known author. This particular multi-published writer of over one hundred novels and short-stories offers a discussion forum at his site, allowing he and fans of his work a unique and personal relationship of sorts. As I read the many posts, the author often revealing his particular writing techniques and preferences, I felt a renewed spark within me concerning my own love of writing. In no way did the topics each of us write about offer any type of remote similarity, but it didn't matter. Our common bond was our need and desire to create via the written word! And so, after a long period of writers block, the mere sight of seeing someone else excited about their work was enough to stir my writing juices back to action!

There are times when I am walking through the woods, and the sight of a simple flower or woodland creature will inspire me. There are also moments when a particular radio or television program will evoke sadness or gladness within me. How fortune we are that God provides so many mediums which allow us the opportunity to stop, look around and see truth for what it is.

Is there some facet of your life that could use some spicing up and refreshing? How about your relationship with God?

I encourage you today to be more aware of ways in which God is trying to reach out to you, so that your spirit may likewise be stirred to new life!

Godly Giving

"But when you give to the needy, do not let your left hand know what your right hand is doing, so that your giving may be in secret. Then your Father, who sees what is done in secret, will reward you." - Matthew 6:3-4

How many people do you know who truly give just for the sake of giving because they know it is good and right to do? How many folks do you know who offer their services, time and emotions, simply because they have a real heart to help a fellow man?

I wish I could say I knew many such people, but, the reality is, few individuals I know give out of a cheerful and loving heart expecting nothing from man or God in return. Even in my own life, while my heart may be acting in love, a small subtle part of me sometimes hopes that God will offer me something in return, such as a prayer answered.

Unfortunately, God does not work this way. When a prayer is answered or a blessing bestowed, our Creator does not issue it as some sort of reward system or trophy for a job well done. No, my friends, God is above such juvenile behavior, and when the Lord gives, He gives because it is good and right to do so.

♥ SON Salutations

The next time you are moved to reach out and give to someone, whether it be volunteering some time to help feed the homeless, work with cancer patients, or offering a supportive shoulder to a friend in need, do so expecting nothing in return, and the simple yet profound joy of knowing you did the right thing because it was the godly thing to do, and not because you would receive earthy recognition, will be all the reward you will need!

God knows, not only our every word and deed, but He knows our true motives behind our actions.

Show God what is in YOUR heart today!

Forgive and Forget

"Remember ye not the former things, neither consider the things of old" -Isaiah 43:18

Have you ever felt very sorry about something you said or did, thus, sought forgiveness from the person you hurt?

At one time or another we all have in-acted in ways that may now make us feel ashamed. This is a result of our limited and often weak human condition. We usually mean well, yet, as human frailty has it, there are often times we need to seek reconciliation with God.

Strangely, even though God has forgiven those of His children who call out to Him in sincere repentance, keeping no record of past wrongs, it is not uncommon for man to dredge up what the Lord has long ago buried. The worst offenders of this are married couples.

We pull out old skeletons from the closet to hurt and humiliate our loved one, and we use long ago resolved issues to further injure and jab. God cleans the slate of those who sincerely repent, yet man tries to over-ride the Divine by playing back past mistakes over and over again like a tired and worn old movie.

What purpose does this serve other than to cause further pain to the person we are attacking?

In all the verbal jabs and blows, there is another "victim." You and I.

Every time we dig up what God has buried, we are, in essence, telling God that our will is more important than His truth. Knowing this, how many of us will still be intent on using the past as a war weapon?

Today, won't you consider making peace with the past by letting it die the death it deserves? Only God could be so good to give us this second chance; this new lease on life! Show your spouse you love him or her by agreeing to never use past mistakes as a future or current judge.

There is only one Judge. His name is God.

Ode to Worried Mothers

As a mother, I know what it is like to be concerned about the health and welfare of my children. However, there are often times I have to remind myself that there is a difference between just concern, and incessant stressing over issues which are fully out of our control, such as a child scraping a knee while playing a game of sports, or a teen enduring rejection from a classmate they have a terrible crush on.

Can needless worry really prevent any of these life circumstances from occurring?

Recently, a relative sent me a poem about worried mothers. The poem spoke of worry as if it was an honored badge to wear, and the time would soon come that we, mom's, would pass the baton down to our children, and so on and so on. The poem which was intended to be a quaint ode to parenting, strangely hit me in an odd way, causing me to reevaluate my role as mother, as well as a believer in God. Two lines of the poem were particularly interesting: "I continued to anguish over their failures, be tormented by their frustrations and absorbed in their disappointments." "Can it be that parents are sentenced to a lifetime of worry?"

♥ SON Salutations

As I pondered such words as "anguish, tormented and frustrations," I was reminded of a story I heard at my first Bible study as a young adult. The lesson that day was faith in God. To drill the instructors point home, he told the class a true story about two mothers. One worried constantly about her young child, and as a result, she suffered many physical ailments related to stress, such as ulcers, nervous jitters, headaches, and the like. The woman's neighbor, another young mother, had a child the same age, yet she never seemed to have such ailments and would go about her daily smiling as she did her chores. In the morning, she'd walk her son to the bus stop, kiss him good bye, wave as he got on the bus, and then she would begin her household chores.

One day, the mother who worried incessantly received a phone call. Her child had been hit by a car, instantly killed by a drunk driver whose car swerved out of control. The two mothers spoke at the funeral, the grieving mother stating through her tears, "I tried to be best mother possible. I warned him about everything as needing to put your gloves on in winter, look both ways before crossing the street, don't run with food in your mouth, and things like that, yet, even though I worried myself sick every time he was out of my sight, look what happened!" The other mother put her hand on the distraught woman's shoulder and quietly said, "As mothers, we do the best we can do, teaching them all we can so they can grow up healthy and happy. Endless worry and stress can not prevent nature from taking its course, and there will be times they come home with scraped knees from playing football, or a broken arm from falling off a bike. Even worry cannot prevent these. The accident was not your fault. It just happened."

The grieving mother listened to her friend, but her words sounded shallow. "If only I had been there, or worried more, perhaps this could have been prevented!" the tearful mother thought.

The grieving mother's neighbor was just as good a mom as anyone else, yet her faith in God called her to place her family's health and welfare in the loving hands of the Lord. Every morning before her husband left for work, and her son prepared to exit for school, she would say a prayer to God to keep her family safe and healthy, leaving worry and fear in God's hands, and not her own. This practice did not ensure that nothing bad would happen to her family, but it allowed her to show God that HE is in control, and that she trusted His wisdom and judgment in all things, even things she herself may not understand.

Today, we have pondered the idea of faith and trust in God. It is not always easy to take something as precious as our family from our own control and place it in to the hands of the Lord, but if we believe in our heavenly Father's abilities, then this form of godly surrender returns its blessings back to us by offering us peace.

God does not require us to be "sentenced" to a joyless existence of physical and emotional "torment" and "frustration," merely because we have children we love.

A loving God would also not wish His children to be plagued with ulcers, nervous jitters, headaches and sour stomachs, or for parents to pass these ailments down to their children.

If you wish to pass down something to your child, offer him wisdom, faith and strength. Let these be his wings, and not fear of living, loving and learning.

Just as you have a child you care about and love, so, too, does God regard YOU as HIS child. He does not harbor fear or anxiety, but rather, His gentle hand is always extended, just waiting for you to grab hold in trust.

A Woman's View of Love

When I reflect on my life thus far, the times in my life I felt most loved was when I felt most safe. I suppose, as a female who is said to be the weaker of the sexes, feeling safe, secure and well-protected is a facet to our genetic makeup. After all, long ago, women relied on men to hunt and skin animals for food, to build their home from massive trees cut down by hand, and to simply be a pillar of strength and character; an example to God and family.

My relationship with my father was no different. As a daughter, I looked up to my father, not just because he was over 6 feet tall, but because, when he was near, I knew everything was OK. He and I would often go for walks in the thick woods near our rural home; him carrying a hand-carved walking stick near his side which I assumed was used to beat any deadly beasts along the way, and I would act as his tiny shadow, listening with great interest as he took his own mental walks down memory lane.

I admired my father due to his gentle and sensible nature, and ability to make those loved ones around him feel safe and secure.

My husband shares many of the same traits as my father, and when we first met, it was not

♥ SON Salutations

long before I felt very secure in his presence. Almost twenty years later, he is still my "rock."

I think it is important to know why we love those we love, and to understand who are the people we respect and admire in our life. Chances are, the qualities we admire or even pursue, tell a great deal about who we are as individuals, and where our priorities lie in the scheme of all things.

There is another person in my life who has been a constant source of strength, comfort and guidance to me, in fact, even more than any individual I have known. When times are good, I know He is always there to share my joy, and when tears well up in my eyes, He is there to comfort me. He is an endless source of wisdom and knowledge, and His strength is beyond human comprehension.

From day one He has been by my side to watch over and care for me, even at those times I may have terribly turned my back on him. Despite it all, He has always been there to forgive and offer the most loving mercy and kindness. Out of all the forms of love I have known in my life, his love surpasses all, and it is within this love I feel safe and secure because I know, without a doubt, I am deeply and completely loved.

♥ SON Salutations

In true love, there is, indeed, great comfort.

The individual I speak about is not spouse, parent, nor even the most attentive friend. His name is Jesus Christ, the Son of God, and I invite you to experience His great love today.

Look To God

Fear

"Fear is our greatest killer. It keeps us from love and hardens the heart." - Chris Griscom

The older I get, the more I am aware of people who seem to be afraid to LIVE. I don't mean to exist, but to really LIVE! If I am fully honest with myself, I must admit that I too am occasionally guilty of this same fear. For example, how many of us can relate to the inner conversations that go on in our heads while having a face-to-face discussion with a new acquaintance? While we are speaking to him or her, our minds are selfishly focusing inward, wondering if we are meeting the approval of the other person, anxious if we appear friendly, intelligent, or appealing enough. What all of this boils down to is fear.

We are afraid to just be ourselves, to let go and allow the simple glory of God shine through and in us. Fear then turns into selfishness and self-centeredness.

Our Heavenly Father does not call us to reach inward, but outward; our hands and hearts reaching in love into the lives of our fellow man. If we are then focusing on our neighbor, suddenly our own worries and stresses no longer seem so overwhelming. We become more loving and giving.

Author Ken Keyes says, "Loving people are happy, and happy people are loving." How true!

Do not let fear zap you of your ability to live joyously, nor to rob you of your salvation in Christ! Call on Him today.

Sun and Rain

After every rain storm eventually comes the sun. Dark and heavy clouds soon give way to bright sky, and before you know it, all traces of storm clouds disappear. Upon smiling at the sun, you wonder how the thunder and lightening could have ever seemed so forbidding.

The above description is true from an earthly perspective; the reality of the change in weather and seasons, yet, did you know the same concept is true, spiritually-speaking?

In the Bible we are told, *"Weeping may endure for a night, but joy cometh in the morning." (Psalm 30:5)* Simply-stated, tears always give way to smiles, but even sorrow must run its course.

In life, we experience a potpourri of emotions. These include, happiness, sadness, anger, and other emotions that may not reflect the best of our character, such as jealousy and envy. While our goal is to find as much peace, joy and contentment as possible, life does not always work that way, and we may find ourselves dealing with meddling mother-in-laws, sibling rivalry, temperamental bosses, and disappointing relationships. The question is, will we allow these bumps or detours in the road to bring us down to the depths of despair, or will we take them in stride, knowing that the darkness will soon give way to the light?

How do we accomplish this seemingly impossible task?

Easy! The answer, my dear friends, is to not focus on the rain-storm, but to instead, cast your attention to the imminent sun.

There is another entity which we may cleave to in times of darkness, and this is the SON of God. Call upon Christ today, and let his love radiate in to your life.

Happiness Now

We seem to face life by holding on to a perfect dream of the future, rather than by seeing the beauty in the current moment. Under this distorted mind set, happiness is never truly in our grasp, but right around the corner, and depending on certain people, places or things.

We tend to view ourselves as works in progress, focusing on the imperfect rather than on what is already good about our total being. We are often quick to beat ourselves up, instead of treating ourselves as kindly as we would treat a total stranger.

Just as God first loved us before we loved Him, before we can reach out to others, we must first learn to cherish ourselves.

Treating yourself lovingly is not an act of conceit or selfishness, but it is an act that teaches us how to be more effective Christians. Again, how can we offer wisdom and understanding to others, if we do not practice it ourselves? How can we preach forgiveness, mercy and love, if we are not willing to apply it to our own daily walk?

Our Heavenly Father did not send His Son,

Jesus Christ, to condemn us for our imperfections, but to offer us salvation by showing us a better way.

Now is the time to stop kicking yourself in the teeth by letting the mistakes of the past weight heavy upon your heart, and instead, to allow His peace and mercy to wash over us in much the same way the ocean waters cleanse the distant shore.

Happiness is not around the corner, because it is right here before us, if only we would open our eyes to the beauty which already exists in every day, hour and moment of our life.

If you need a helping hand to see this, then just call on God today.

The Ocean

The ocean has always been a special place for me; a place to let nature soothe my mind, allowing it's waters to refresh and awaken my senses, and the rhythm of the surf to revive my soul in the same way one's heart brings life blood into their veins. While the mountains are also a favorite escape of mine, there is just something unique about the tropical sun and surf that draws me again and again to the cool and crystal blue waters of the ocean.

Where is your special vacation or relaxation spot; the place where you can rest and recoup? For some people, it is a wilderness trip or exhilarating hike up the side of a mountain. The splendid glory of tall pines, field flowers and clean air intoxicates your eyes and lungs, and it is not long before worry becomes nothing more than a distant memory.

Or perhaps your escape is to canoe down a winding river, stopping occasionally to dip your toes in the quenching water?

Many people even find similar solitude in their own back yard. Just tie up a hammock, grab a good book, and glass of ice cold mint tea, and, voila! Instant oasis!

God gave mankind nature to be enjoyed and used to our godly advantage, but let us not forget that there is a supreme refuge in our heavenly Father. In His Divine presence we may not only find peace, comfort and joy, but as do those cool waters of the ocean crash over ones body, so too, does His mercy and grace purify those of us who seek truth.

Open your eyes to the beauty around you, including, God.

Musings On Death

I've been thinking about life and death. While most people view thoughts on life to be quite joyous, pondering death seems to have taken a bad rap.

Ask a teen to draw a picture of death, and I'll bet you many of them will scrawl skeletons, blood-soaked weapons, decayed bodies, and other morbid artifacts that are typically shown in most Hollywood horror flicks.

How accurate a mental image is this, though?

As I am now a woman in my forties, I have come to better appreciate life. While it is my hope and desire to live to a ripe old age, no one ever knows for certain when their number will be called. I try to live my days well, ever thankful for the time the Lord has already given me on this beautiful planet, and grateful for my health, friends and loved ones.

Interestingly, even though I am still quite young and in excellent health, I have already made peace with death. I know it is unavoidable, so the best I can do is accept its inevitability and think optimistically about it. After all, what most people fear about death is its uncertainty.

From the moment we take our first breath of life as new born babe, sickness, disease, injury and death is a possibility we face every day. We've all read the stories where some man is taking his morning jog, and bam! He falls over from a heart attack. Or what about the eighteen year old female who was just diagnosed with AIDS, or the mother of five children whose Multiple Sclerosis is so bad that
she can no longer physically care for her children?

Not only are we uncertain about how and when we will die, LIFE, itself, is an uncertainty! For example, we
marry with every intention of being blissfully happy together forever, but sometimes, things simply don't turn out that way, or we lose our job, trip and break an ankle, and, well, I think you get the picture. In fact, statistically,
LIFE is much more unpredictable than death!

When my time comes, I will look death straight in the eye and spit at it, and while I am doing that, I will be reaching out to the good Lord to lead me safely and gently back home where I belong in His love and care.

My faith allows me to have confidence in my salvation, but what about those people who do not know God's goodness?

♥ SON Salutations

Rather than ponder death, let us be glad for LIFE, which includes God's promise of eternal life.

Let all you do be done in love.

I Corinthians 16:14

Peaceful Beginnings

"Peace is always beautiful." - Walt Whitman

I start most of my days with peaceful beginnings. What are "peaceful beginnings," you ask?

Well, in simple terms, it is starting the morning off with my spirit being calmed rather than stressfully churned. It is beginning the day with a smile, instead of a scowl, and a spring in my step, rather than dragging my legs as if the weight of the world were upon my shoulders.

For me, peaceful beginnings also include standing on my balcony, and taking a deep breath of fresh air, glad for life, all its blessings, and especially, at that moment, for the familiar smell of coffee as it meets the warm summer air. Often times, I will break the morning silence by putting on a special CD of gentle harp, classical or world music.

I do all of this because it is my desire to live happily and well. I have chosen to seek peace in mind, body and spirit because God calls those who believe in Him to be peacemakers. If we are at war within ourselves, how can we then have joy?

The answer, my friends, is to call upon the Lord, and place Him within your heart, and then do your best to seek those things which are truly beautiful; which edify and feed the spirit, rather than detract from it. By feeding our spirit with God, and nourishing our minds and bodies with those things that bring peace, then we may truly be called peacemakers.

Enjoy Life

"Life is an ecstasy." - Emerson

When I read the quote by Emerson, I had to stop and ponder its accuracy. While I certainly have heard many a person refer to life as a most precious gift, would most people classify their existence as "ecstasy?" After all, I don't know about you, but that particular word conjures up images of sheer bliss and ultimate nirvana, if such a state is indeed possible.

Just when I was ready to reject the author's conclusion, it occurred to me that if life is, indeed, what you make of it, then why can't we choose bliss over mediocrity, and joy over complacency? I then began to recall that just a few short weeks ago, as I was grilling our dinner outside, I was surprised by how much pleasure I gained from such a simple scene as being surrounded by my family, as we all talked and laughed while sitting around our picnic table. The smell of pine from the trees, and the steak and peppers on the grill were an intoxicating delight to breathe in!

It's amazing the small things we can find delight in, isn't it? Whether it's a stroll in the woods, a midnight viewing of the stars, or the pleasure one feels when they run in to an old friend in the mall, life can be an ecstasy if we learn to make the most out of each moment of every day. However, earthly happiness only goes so far, and the most fulfilling joy can only be found in, not only godly living, but God, Himself.

Those who are truly wise will seek God first, and the happiness that comes from good honest living will fall in to place naturally.

Procrastinating

"Never leave that till tomorrow which you can today." - Benjamin Franklin

Sometimes, it seems like there are simply not enough hours in the day. I start off the day with the best of intentions, and by time evening rolls around, there are many instances where I do not accomplish all I had planned.

I'm sure this happens to all of us at one time or another, but what about procrastinating in the long-term sense? Here's an example.

For the past year, I've been atypically lax in my regular exercise routine. I used to hit the gym just about every day, even adding regular daily
walks in the evenings with my dog, but I've strayed so far from my original intent of keeping firm and fit, that I, admittedly, have gained a few pounds. I am very displeased over this, and lately, I've been promising myself f I will begin this day anew, but by time I rest my head on my pillow at night, I am again disappointed I did not live up to my goal.

What about you? Do you ever promise yourself that tomorrow will be a better day, yet when tomorrow comes, nothing changes? Before long, a day turns in to a week, and a week turns in to a month, and months turn in to a year! The sad part is, what happens when a year turns in to a lifetime?

This inspirational is not just about putting off chores and errands, but about procrastinating with our spirituality.

Whether you are already a person of faith who has fallen in to a path of ungodliness, or a seeking individual who has kept running away from a relationship with God, time always eventually catches up to us. We may procrastinate regarding our salvation, but the consequences for doing so will be devastating.

Out of Shape

Since this past summer, I've encountered more difficult situations in that short time, than I have in the past several years. Within the last six months, I came down with a non-life threatening yet irritating virus which constantly left me weak and tired. My son was also in and out of the hospital with unexplained continual vomiting and weight loss, so, of course, despite my own physical state, I was right there by his side to sleep in a spare hospital bed next to his. I've also been dealing with two very hormonal teens who seem to be in the midst of teenage rebellion, not to mention, two family members who recently announced they are getting a divorce.

I should know from experience that, during these stressful times, is when I need to ensure my mind, body, and spirit connection is even more strong, but, sad to say, I did just the opposite, allowing myself to fall terribly out of shape. Not only did I break from my gym routine, but I also even stopped my daily walks. It's not that I gained so much weight; only a few pounds actually, but I feel my decline in health most in my muscles, which are no longer strong and firm, but soft and mushy.

While I don't feel emotionally eager to hit the gym, deep down in my heart, I know it is exactly what I need to get those juices flowing and muscles pumping.

So, today, I'm going to stuff my shorts and bathing suit in to my gym bag, and force my self back to health. I know it will be hard, and my muscles will scream every step of the way, but I have no one to blame but myself.

Funny how easy it is to fall out of shape isn't it? Keep in mind, I am not solely referring to physical shape, either, but emotional and spiritual shape as well.

As you can see from my own above revelation, just as a state of ill-health can subtly creep up on you if you are not careful, so too, can small neglects and bad choices pull us farther away from a fulfilling relationship with God.

Thankfully, I am only left to roll my eyes at some flabby thighs and arms, but what about the folks who sink so low in to ungodliness, that their spirit suffers an even more devastating loss?

It is not too late to hit the gym, and it is not too late to call out to God.

Unexpected Results

Have you ever endured a difficult situation, certain its outcome will be undesirable, and then lo-and-behold, what you dreaded, turned out to be a blessing in disguise?

A while back, I wrote an inspirational about a similar past event in my own life. I was very distraught over the breakup of my very first boyfriend who I had given several years of my life. I pleaded with God to mend our relationship, but such was not the case. Over twenty-two years later, I can honestly look back and be overjoyed for the ending of that relationship, knowing that had we married, it would have been a relationship doomed to fail. We were simply two different people on two distinct paths.

This is not the first time, what originally was perceived as a "negative" turned out to instead be a "positive." In fact, there have been many times in my life when that proverbial door was closed, and in its place, a window was opened, allowing some wonderful opportunity to me mine. For example, many years ago, my husband lost his job due to no fault of his own. What could have been a terrible hardship, instead turned in to a rare opportunity! You see, it was our dream to move to a home in the mountains, but what was preventing us was my husband's job. Now, with the loss of his job, there was nothing holding us back, so we packed our bags and relocated to a most beautiful area of the Rocky Mountains. Sure, times were financially tough as my husband had to look for another job, but, so many years later, we now look back and agree they were the best times we had as a family!

Interesting how things always seem to iron themselves out when God is on your side.

All of these situations have proved to me that God is always watching over us. Like a loving and attentive Father, our Creator desires our ultimate health and well-being, so why do so many people fear to place their faith in the caring hands of God? I can only guess, they simply don't know how good God is.

Today, why don't you take a leap of faith, and give God a try? The end result just might surprise you.

Anger Management

*"If you are patient in one moment of anger,
you will escape a hundred days of sorrow."*
 -Chinese Proverb

I don't know about you, but I've always had a hard time understanding people who have difficultly controlling their anger, thus, easily lose their temper. I've had the displeasure of working beside some folks like this, who huff and puff whenever the going gets a little tough, and I am always reminded of a child who is having a temper tantrum. You know the type. A child can't get his own way so he whines, screams, kicks his heals, pounds his fists, and generally makes certain no one around him is having a good time. With a child, such an act is more tolerable since you tend to chalk it up to immaturity, but with an adult, shouldn't they know better by now?

As the above ancient proverb implies, the inability to control temper goes far beyond the moment of anger. Thoughtless and hurtful words said in haste, can often jab deep to the core of those we love, respect, and consider dear friends. The shouting may have ended, but those hurtful words can last a lifetime.

No, I do not understand people who lash out

with angry words when stressed, but then again, I do not understand my own flaws either.

We all have them, you know. Those irritating little things about ourselves that we really would like to change; those character traits that we are less than proud of.

No man is spared from his humanity, but through God, we can reach through our natural self, and gain sight of a more beautiful spiritual realm. Alone, we may not be able to do it, but with God, ALL things are possible! By my self, I am weak, but with God, I am strong. Without the Creator, I struggle with my weaknesses, but my faith in Him allows my course to be set straight once again!

There may be times man disappoints me, but my Heavenly Father's love is always enduring.

Yes, love does endure, and that is why, if you have hurt someone through your words or deeds, only love can undo the wicked sting.

Reach out your hand to God, and you will not be alone.

Simple Things

Funny. Seems like the more life gets complicated, the more I appreciate the simple things. In case you're not sure what I mean, I'm referring to those little things in life we often brush off, failing to recognize the importance of such things as an hour of peace and quiet, a steeping cup of our favorite herb tea, a relaxing hot bath with no interruptions, a good book, fresh, crisp bed sheets, a good belly laugh, or a tasty home-cooked meal.

Perhaps the wisdom that often comes with age has allowed me to see what is significant, and what is mere lip service, fluff, and vanity. If this is the case, then thank goodness for every new wrinkle I receive, for I would gladly exchange youthful hair or skin for the ability to live better and love more.

What good is outer beauty if there is no one to share all the blessings and joys life has to offer? What purpose does joy have if we are too blind to see it?

In my own life, one simple thing that I have always valued was cooking our evening dinner. Certainly, there are those days I'm too tired to cook, or simply don't feel like putting a whole lot of effort in to it, but, in general, I've always gotten a certain degree of satisfaction from cooking for my family. I suppose it sounds silly, but I've always felt that if my husband can work hard all day, the least I can do is to offer him something tasty to come home to.

For me, cooking dinner is about more than just putting food on the table It is an act of love and self that takes time and energy to give. This is exactly what I mean about appreciating the small things.

How many people today will simply eat to fill their belly, not really appreciating the effort put in to the act? How many people will eat supper today and give no thought whatsoever to the millions of people in Third World countries who have no food to eat? Ah, the things we take for granted.

Life can be so good if only we open our eyes to its many joys.

In similar manner, our relationship with God is another aspect of life we often overlook, yet critically need! Call on Him today!

Goldfish

How many of us live the life of a goldfish?

Sounds silly?

Not really.

Think about it. A goldfish lives in the limited space of his bowl, looking out at the world. Sad to say, many people live a similar existence, remaining in their safe, limited realms, afraid to reach out in to territories unexplored; especially, the uncharted terrain of relationships. People come in and out of their life, unfazed and untouched by the wonderful gifts that lie deep in store each of us, if only we would take the time to let them be opened.

I'd much rather think that we are called to be as butterflies, opening our wings and letting all men see the beauty that resides in our hearts.

In similar manner, when it is dark and we have a candle, do we hide the candle under a rock, or use its light so that others may see?

Just as our talents and gifts of self are to be utilized and shared for the benefit of others, so too, does Christ call us to not hide His good

♥ SON Salutations

news. This message is that God offers us the gift of salvation which is ours for the taking.

Receive your gift today and don't be a goldfish.

A Lesson on Faith

There are certain laws of physics that we know exist. For example, toss an apple up in the air and what happens? The law of gravity determines that what goes up must come down, of course!

Did you know there are also spiritual laws? That's right. One of these divinely-appointed principles is that what we sow, so shall we also reap. In more plain terms, if we are hateful and sow seeds of scorn and malice, we will obviously not reap joy, peace, and love.

In like manner, if we scatter seeds of understanding, patience, and kindness, should we expect anything less than good gifts? The same is true with how we chose to live our life; not only what comes out of our mouth, but what do our actions reveal; godliness or that which is objectionable to God? Again, in more clear terms, if we are involved in something as sinful as adultery, should we expect God to bless our marriage? Our Lord may want to see us truly blessed, but if we are not willing to place our faith, trust and obedience in His hands, this cannot occur.

Our faith in God is about more than simply loving God and having a relationship with

Him.

Just as when we marry, we say an earthly vow to honor our commitment to one spouse, the same is true with the commitment and obedience God requires us to have with Him. This does not mean there is not forgiveness to those who stumble or fall, but what it does mean is, what good is our faith if we only adhere to that which is convenient, pleasing, and tolerable? Even the unsaved heathens can manage that!

Christians are not called to be as unrepentant heathens, but we are instead called to be as light to a world of darkness. This too, is another spiritual principle, that obedience to God IS rewarded. Our faith is never in vain, and its reward is salvation!

I'm Sorry

As an adolescent, I had a difficult time saying "I'm sorry," most likely because it was never taught to me how important these two little words are. Thanks to a good friend, I later learned this most valuable lesson, and applied it whenever I inadvertently hurt a loved one's feelings with an insensitive comment, an unkind deed, or a major screw-up.

The profound affect this seemingly insignificant phrase can have as it touches the heart of another is something worth, not only exploring, but teaching our children.

The words, "I'm sorry," can erase years of pent up bitterness, and act as a soothing balm to the injured heart of the person who needs to hear these words.

The phrase, "I'm sorry," is not something we do just for the "other person," but we do it for ourselves, and for God, so that we do not carry negative emotional and spiritual baggage that may cause us to harbor guilt, bitterness, resentment, or strained friend and family ties. These few words spoken in less than a few seconds, show the person we have injured, whether purposely or not, that the pain they are experiencing, is important to us, and it is our desire to help lessen that heavy load.

Saying, "I'm sorry," is a gift of love and personal responsibility because it enables us to come face to face with our mistakes, as well as validates the other persons pain. To fail to acknowledge the hurt of another human being is similar to walking by the scene of an accident and doing nothing while a fellow man suffers. There is no difference to God if we ignore a man bleeding and dying in the street, or turn our nose up at the emotional hurts of another human being.

Of the many lessons the Bible teaches, the practice of repentance is stressed. While God forgives those who seek His mercy, He does not offer forgiveness to those who refuse to admit their sins or attempt to hide the true contents of their heart from our Heavenly Father's ever-watchful eye. God cannot forgive the unrepentant, and if we do not forgive others, God will not forgive us.

Today, as you ponder this lesson, won't you consider open corners in your own life that could benefit from the healing words of "I'm sorry?"

This includes things we may have done against

our fellow man, as well as to God.

As our heavenly Father, God is rich with mercy to those who set pride aside and humbly approach Him, but unless we reach out and take hold of His always extended hand, we will forever carry our sinful burdens like a heavy bag of bricks that sets upon our back to weight us emotionally down, and rob us of our spiritual salvation.

Lessen your load. Call on Christ today.

The Key to Happiness

"Happiness is a conscious choice, not an automatic response." -Mildred Barthel

Much has been written by various authors about happiness. For example, as the above writer conveys, a general feeling of wellness is not something that just happens to us with no work on our part, but takes a very real conscious decision and daily commitment.

As I tell my friends, each day when we awake, we have two plates before us. One plate is filled with bitterness, pessimism, and scorn. The other plate is filled with laughter, smiles, appreciation and optimism. Which ever plate you select for your first meal of the day tends to determine your demeanor and outlook, so be careful what you put in your mouth because you ARE what you eat!

According to Maria Luisa-Bombal, most people have an unrealistic picture of what happiness is supposed to "feel" like, and that by expecting something grander or bigger than life, true happiness often passes us by unrecognized. The author suggests we slow down and appreciate all the small pleasures in life, and then we will better notice happiness. Here is what she says, "It may be true that happiness lies in the conviction that one has irremediably lost happiness. Then we can begin to move through life without hope or fear, capable of finally enjoying all the small pleasures, which are the most lasting."

Perhaps due to an increase of infidelity in marriage, Douglas Jerrold wisely encourages his listeners to seek happiness only in their own yards. He states, "Happiness grows at own firesides, and is not to be picked in stranger's gardens."

More words of wisdom are offered by Doris Mortmon, "Until you make peace with who you are, you'll never be content with what you have."

According to this Chinese proverb, happiness is not found internally, but externally. "If you want happiness for an hour, take a nap. If you want happiness for a day, go fishing. If you want happiness for a month, get married. If you want happiness for a year, inherit a fortune. If you want happiness for a lifetime, help someone else."

In my opinion, there are two secular authors who sum up the meaning of happiness best. These writers are Victor Hugo and Allan Chalmers. In the pursuit of happiness, both of

these men recognize the supreme significance of love and meaningful life purpose.
"The grand essentials of happiness are: something to do, something to love, and something to hope for." - Allan Chalmers

"The supreme happiness of life is the conviction that we are loved." - Victor Hugo

While I am certain there are endless quotations, poems and essays on true happiness, it seems clear that this general sentiment of well-being that we call happiness, is not an external, but internal phenomenon whose foundation is steeped in godliness. So, if God is indeed, love, then how can we truly know love unless we have a relationship with the Divine? How can we wish to seek goodness if we do not possess godly wisdom?

Small pleasures can indeed be found in the most simple things as a shared laugh with a friend, or a relaxing cup of tea and good book, but the most fulfilling joy can only come from knowledge that we are in God's good graces, and that we have reached out of ourselves to share this precious gift with others.

Circle of Life

"The poppies illustrate the "Circle of life." Seeds flourish, maturing to full bloom, transforming to pods, which scatter more seeds. Make the most of your circle!" -Peg Conley

As Peg Conley conveys, life is an unceasing process of change. Just as the seeds of the poppy fall back to the earth, only to flourish yet again, so too, will the proverbial circle of life touch our own existence. Hardships may indeed befall us, but the ebb and flow of life energy prods us to survive. Whether we are experiencing the death of a loved one, an ended relationship, or grief for the past, as incomprehensible as it may seem, life DOES go on.

How do I know this?

Open your window wide and look outside. The sun still rises and sets, stars still shine, people are on their way to work and play.

Troubling circumstances and heart-wrenching situations may inwardly tear at our heart and cause us to feel like crumbling, but let us not forget that even in cemeteries grow flowers, grass and trees. Death, be it in the loss of friend or loved one, or mourning for a relationship

failed, indeed has its sting, but as long
as Christ promises us hope, life shall not cease.
God's grace is as a healing hand.

In the Bible, the book of Ecclesiastes (Chapter 3, Verse 1) reveals that *"To everything there is a season, and a time to every purpose under the sun. A time to be born, and a time to die; a time to plant, and a time to pluck up that which is planted..."*

Indeed there is a time to mourn, but there is also a time for tears to dry. As does the sweet scent of the poppy linger in the air, the warm memories and love for those we have lost will remain always safe in our hearts.

Life is about living, and that is why God offered us His Son, so that we may have eternal life. A life without Christ will rob one of salvation, but with Him, all
things are possible!

Mother's Work

They say, "A woman's work is never done." Most people over the age of thirty-five know this phrase signifies that, for mother's, there is always something to do. Whether it is cooking, cleaning, putting band-aids on scraped knees, going to PTA meetings, or playing taxi while you drive a mini-van filled with kids to the movies or roller-skating, the role of "mother" is hardly a 9-5 job.

Never before have I felt the tug of 24-7 parental commitment, than at this point in my own children's life; the trying teenage years. While some teens fly through this hormonal and emotional period with a breeze, many teenagers and their families endure great moments of stress that would try even the patience of Job.

A mother in this same predicament wrote, asking me if I had any advice to offer her. From what her letter revealed, their house had become more a war ground, than "home sweet home." My advice was to continue to love and pray daily for her children, something we often forget to do when we don't "feel" like it.

When times are tough, and it appears we have exhausted all our options; pray. When anger

♥ SON Salutations

and frustration is infiltrating your mind, dig down deep and remember the love and commitment. When warm and fuzzy emotions feel far from the surface, call out to God and let Him remind you that you are loved, and so too, are you called to love.

Perhaps today's inspirational is not what you expected, but the reality is, not all families are currently running as smooth a level of operation as that revealed on the old 50's sitcom, "Leave It To Beaver." Not all mothers are standing in front of their stoves today, dressed in pearls and high heels, gleaming a smile that continually radiates the joys of motherhood, while they baste a ham. Likewise, our children are not always sweet and mannerly. The truth is, some mothers will not be issued any type of recognition, even on Mother's Day. There will be no boxes of candy, or fragrant corsages, or hand-drawn cards of crayon.

Today's meditation is for such mothers; the ones who have given selflessly and to the best of their abilities. No one said motherhood would be easy, and just as we endured the messy diapers, sleepless nights cradling a feverish child in our arms, and dealing with the "Terrible Twos," with little or no recognition, so too will these trying moments pass. When it happens, we will look back and say, "yes, it was difficult at times, but this is exactly what being a mom is all about; enduring the hard times along with the good times, just like marriage, for better or worse, sickness and health."

Recognition might not come today in the form of cards or flowers, but it will come from deep inside you; from knowing you have done a job well done.

It is true, a mother's work is never done. As long as our hearts are beating, and our lungs are working, our job will never end. As does God love us 24-7, so too is this esteemed role of motherhood.

Nobody is a Nobody

This is a true story about a boy who, the world might say, was a terrible underachiever. While in the eighth grade, he failed subjects repeatedly. High school wasn't much better; he flunked Latin, algebra, English, and received a grade of zero in physics.
The boy managed to make the school golf team, but he lost the most important golf match of the season, and even though there was a consolation match, he failed miserably in that too. It's not that his peers disliked this boy; it's just that they never really seemed to notice him much. Even "Hellos" in the hall were a rarity.

Out of all the failures in his life, there was something that did hold great importance to this boy, his love of drawing. Although in high school, the cartoons he submitted to the yearbook were rejected, once out of school, the boy was so sure of his artistic talent that he approached Walt Disney Studios with drawing samples. I wish I could say the studio execs loved his work and immediately hired him, but such was not the case another huge rejection.

Despite his many lack of successes, this boy did not give up. He then decided to write his own autobiography in cartoons, about a little boy who was regarded as a loser and nobody. The name of this boy was Charles Schulz, the creator of the famous Charlie Brown and Peanuts comic strip.

In life, it is sometimes easy to feel like a nobody. We pass hundreds of people on the street on our way to work, or walk through a faceless crowd in a mall, and no one seems to notice or care. Deep inside, we may know we are special and unique and have lots to offer, but unless someone takes the time to look our way and give us a chance, we may feel worthless and mediocre, just like Charlie Brown who couldn't even manage to fly a kite or kick a football properly.

Just as Charles Schulz had faith in his artistic talent, so too, must we realize that nobody is a nobody... especially in God's eyes. We all have special gifts and talents, and every human being is deserving and capable of being loved and appreciated.

Today, I invite you to look deep within yourself, and rather than see what you can do to improve yourself, as all the many self-help books suggest, find what you already "like" about yourself!

♥ SON Salutations

Do you have an awesome laugh or smile? Are you thoughtful and sensitive to the needs of others? Are you down-to-earth and practical? Do you enjoy your ability to dream and hope?

Our heavenly Father does not see with external eyes, but sees to the very core of our foundation. There is nothing we can hide from Him, and He alone, knows our motives and most secret desires. Learn to love yourself the way our Creator does, and learn to reach out to others the same way God is awaiting you with open arms.

Out Of Whack

We all know how various forms of machinery such as a pop or candy machine, can get out of whack, thus be in need of professional repair, but did you know your life could become just as easily off kilter? Sometimes, all we need is a good jolt to set us back on the right path, similar to how some people give a faulty coin-operated machine a good wrap.

We become imbalanced when we allow ourselves to be so heavily involved in a particular corner of life that the scales subtly begin to lean in favor of this one issue, often, allowing this topic to dominate our thoughts, even actions.

How many people do you know that are workaholics? Even something as necessary and noble as "work" can slowly turn a good thing in to a medium that allows parent to child communication to be hindered, wives to become frustrated and embittered over a spouse who is never there, and a husband who begins to perceive his only purpose in life as that of provider. "Work" has thus replaced joy, laughter, sharing and intimacy.

What about fantasy and dreams? God made

♥ SON Salutations

man with a brain that is capable of awesome intellectual abilities, including our ability to imagine, but what happens when this gift is continually misused, such as in the case of sexual fantasy with someone other than your spouse? The woman in the below story can answer that.

Although Laurie had been married with children for many years, she never fully emotionally let go of the love she had for an old flame. When times grew stressful in her own marriage, Laurie would sink deep within her thoughts, envisioning exotic getaways with her "dream man." "Dream" is right, for that is exactly what it was; a figment on her own imagination. If truth be-known, while Laurie held a secret torch for this past love, in "his" mind, Laurie was nothing more than a distant memory.

What part of "your" life might be out of whack due to some sort of imbalance as obsessive hungers, ungodly thought processes, or the scales of work or play leaning too heavily in one direction? Can you see how these behaviors are not helping, but hurting you; physically, emotionally, even spiritually?

In the above story, what Laurie perceived as harmless fantasy, was not so harmless after all.

Her many years of comparison; measuring her former flame to her current husband, had not only furthered her frustrations, but caused her very spirit to be divided. No longer did her spouse have her "all," but a piece of her was always with another man.

Had she continued on this way, chances are, Laurie's marriage would be doomed to fail. Just as that old pop or candy machine sometimes needs a good kick in the side, so too, do we sometimes need a jolt of hard reality. Some people do not face this reality until it's too late or there is a death, sickness or traumatic life circumstance, but thankfully, a relationship with God can be the most continuous wake-up call! Getting in to the habit of daily communication (prayer), with the Creator, is one of the best ways to remind ourselves to keep that scale straight, and with God in the center.

Godly Understanding

Why do bad things sometimes happen to good people?

I wish I had some deeply intellectual and rational answer, but the truth of the matter is, No man does. Sometimes, despite our most fervent efforts to eat healthy and exercise, ill health still befalls us, and regardless of how safe a driver we may be, in the blink of an eye, a traffic accident can send us to the hospital. If you want to take a short trip to the loony bin, then try to understand why innocent children can be abducted from the safety of their own yards, why great men in leadership may be assassinated, and why seemingly decent people do stupid things like steal, hate, commit adultery, lie, and dishonor their parents.

The older I get, and hopefully, the wiser, the less I try to understand why. Sure, we can speculate and hypothesize, but when all is said and done, only God truly knows what exists in the hearts and minds of men.

I try to do the best I can do in all things, and then I let the pieces fall where they may under the ever-watchful eye of the Lord. That is really all we CAN do. We cannot control the minds and actions of others, nor can we turn back the hands of time.

It certainly seems we cannot control much in our life, doesn't it?

Ah, nothing could be farther from the truth! While we may not be able to control others, we CAN learn to better keep reigns on our own actions. We can also undo great heartbreaks by forgiving those who seek forgiveness, and for releasing our own hatred when justice does not seem to prevail. While we may not be able to undo sinful actions that have already past, we can control the words that leave our mouth in the present, as well as vow to keep our own ever-mindful eye on the future.

No, we cannot understand all things, nor can we rewind the great hands of time, but with a little bit of godly understanding, life can indeed be sweeter.

Anything For Love

There is a song by the recording artist, "Meatloaf", titled, "I Would Do Anything For Love."

It is true that love is a grand thing to pursue, and we are also called by God TO love, but sadly, sometimes in our struggle to give and receive love, we find ourselves on an entirely different path.

In the name of "love," marriages in crisis are often destroyed as lust is mistaken for love.

Oftentimes, jealousy and possessiveness masquerades as love. In the pursuit of love, sometimes we leap before seeing what is on the other side of the cliff.

What would you do to have real love? Climb a mountain? Swim an ocean? Cut off one of your limbs?

We may think such drastic measures must be taken to find true love, but right around the corner; in fact, right in front of our very eyes, exists that most precious treasure! Unfortunately, many of us walk right by it because we are expecting it to look and feel the same way love is often presented in made-for-television movies and cheap romantic novels.

Certainly, there is something to say for romance and passion, but let us not confuse one for the other. Love is not something you can hold or see, for it is purely internal and outside of the earthly natural realm. It is not blonde or brunette, or possessing certain dimensions, nor is it measured by the size of one's pocketbook or titles of prestige.

True love comes from one place, and one place only. God. Unless we seek the Lord first, chances are, we will never fully understand or recognize true love, because the foundation of love is built upon God.

♥ SON Salutations

A Deeper Hunger

Have you ever had a hunger for a certain food? You know, on those days you just have to have a sweet, such as a donut or chocolate sundae. What about the times you crave a salty or crunchy food item, such as potato chips or peanuts?

The same thing is true with our physical bodies. Sometimes, our body just seems to crave to be held, scratched or loved. These are all very normal physical needs, but did you know that because God created us as spiritual beings with a deeper purpose, we have very real spiritual cravings as well? That's right. The sad part is that lots of people feel these spiritual hunger pangs and aren't sure what to do about it. They try to load the spiritual calling with fillers that offer temporary good feelings, but the reality is, they only offer "empty calories," and their flavor leaves a bitter aftertaste.

How many people do you know that try to fill this void with sex, drugs, alcohol, and keeping their life so full of activity they don't have time to think about meaty spiritual substance? Are these people happy as they outwardly appear, or when they are alone and in the privacy of their own home, are their hearts inwardly filled with despair?

There IS a food that is sweet to the taste, and truly fulfilling and satisfying, and this substance is the bread of life that only God can offer through His living word.

What is His living word? It is the truth that lives within Him, and anyone who believes in Him, and is reflected in how we live our daily life. Will the actions we carry out in our life reflect godliness, or will our day to day actions and thoughts be tainted with sin?

Just as you listen to your body when it has an itch, and you offer it a nice scratch, won't you listen to your hungry spirit as it calls out for God?

Bogged Down

Imagine swimming in a lovely pond surrounded by the beauty of nature. Floral bouquets fill the air, as does the sweet scent of newly mown grass. A tiny green frog jumps in at the ponds edge; he too, is enjoying the warm glow of the summer sun. Swimming gracefully, your arms move like those of a seasoned ballerina.

All is well with the world, and a sense of peace permeates your entire being. Without notice, a strand of thick seaweed brushes against your leg. "Odd," you think, "I don't recall seaweed ever being here before." And so, you continue to swim on, paying little attention to each green feathery fiber that now clings to your limbs in much the same way lint gathers on a wool skirt. Before long, your legs can no longer flutter through the water as well because the weight of the seaweed has become so great that movement is now hindered. Suddenly you panic and wonder how you could have been so blind to not see the danger before you. Thankfully, you are able to free yourself before anything life-threatening occurs, but, scared and shaking, you vow to be much more cautious when swimming.

Think of how often the same act occurs in our

lives. We get so involved in work, socializing, and family life, that it is easy to get bogged down with dozens of small stresses. Alone, the stresses are easy to cope with, but when multiplied, become as a heavy weight upon your back which not only have the capacity to pull you emotionally and physically down, but to also carry you farther away from God.

Life can indeed be sweet; as pleasant as that summer swim in the pond, but let us also keep our eyes open to the potential dangers around us so that we do not find ourselves in the danger zone of separation from God. Sin can creep up on us as subtly as a snake slithers in the grass, and a too full schedule can turn our heads away from what is truly important; our walk with God.

Balancing Act

At various points in my life I allowed the scales to tip too much to one side. For example, as a teen, there was time I was so "in" to my friends, that I didn't put much time and effort in to my parents and siblings. As I grew older, I recall a serious relationship I was so wrapped up in that my friends grew concerned with why I stopped calling and socializing. At yet another time, being over-involved in a project forced me to neglect my important role as a caring and attentive parent.

Even now, I occasionally fall in to strong temporary mind-sets that make that invisible scale lean too heavily to one side. Upon realizing the "tilt," I ponder the word that has kept me focused all these many years.

Giving all of our emotions and energy to something as, say, parenting, may seem like a noble thing, but keep in mind, that while children may greatly benefit from such an attentive and giving parent, there is also someone who will be neglected.

Thanks to the most recent medical information, we now know that parents need "time-outs" too, to regroup, de-stress, and take care of our own needs as well as our children's. When "we" are healthy and balanced in mind-body-spirit, so too, may our little one's reap the rewards!

The same is true with our relationship with God. How often to we let the scale tip as we place job, social life, and various other projects and interests BEFORE our walk with our Creator? If we take care of mind and body, yet neglect spirit, where is the balance?

While joy is eternal, obtaining a balance in life may bring more happiness and fulfillment to your soul. One thing is for sure, the reward for inviting Christ in to your life is salvation.

Consider the Lilies of the Field

We Both Wear Pants

Donald and Doris were at the end of their rope. They had tried all the latest marital gimmicks, and now, here they were sitting in a counselors office, one step away from divorce. "I don't know what it is about, Doris," shouted Donald, "She takes everything so personally! I forget something as little as our anniversary and she bursts in to tears!" "The problem is Donald, not me! He is unromantic, doesn't talk, and only cares about fishing, camping and cars," retorted an infuriated Doris.

The remainder of the story, you can most likely figure out. After a few hours of letting off steam, the marriage counselor soon enlightens Doris and Donald on the differences in the sexes, and how these unique characteristics dramatically affect, not only how we communicate, but how we understand or perceive ourselves and others. Once this couple better understands these differences, they will then have a better chance of working through issues in a more clear light.

While male and female may now both wear pants, that is about as far as our "sameness" goes. Sure, we women have come a long way in our fight for equality, but, there are some things that we just cannot change, try as we may.

Setting emotional differences aside, let's look for a moment at the physical differences in male and female.

The female body is composed of more fat than males. Not only does fat in all the right places give us a more curvy and feminine look, but the fat actually serves a purpose in the whole process of childbearing and nursing. The male body, on the other hand, tends to be more muscular and angular, and, unlike most females, men tend to have more hair on their body, even in places we, females, have no desire to grow follicles, such as on the back, chest, and ears! Regarding voice tones, men's voices tend to run deeper and richer than the higher pitch of the female. While there are definite emotional differences between the sexes, one of these differences stems from the very simple fact females have a menstrual cycle and men don't. The altering of hormones during this period of time is known for leaving most women feeling weary, weepy, crabby and sleepy, not to mention bloated due to water-retention, a common ailment that often goes hand in hand with PMS. Emotionally, it doesn't take a rocket scientist to figure out that, on the whole, women tend to

♥ SON Salutations

Be more emotional than men. For starters, young males are taught that it's not masculine to cry, and if a spider crawls on their knee, it looks wimpy if they run out of the room screaming, "EEEEK!" When a woman is upset and frustrated, in many cases she will hysterically cry, but when a man is upset, chances are he will either pound a wall, or become VERY silent, withdrawing to that emotional dark cave in his mind. And what is the first thing we, females, want to do when we see a problem? Let's talk it out and have a deep discussion! What women call trying to get him to open up and communicate, men call nagging!

With all these differences, it's amazing male and female can ever hook up! Alas, we do manage, but the differences are still with us, even for the closest of soul mates.

The reason it is imperative we understand the differences in the sexes is boiled down to one simple word: Communication.

Whether we are communicating with spouse, next door neighbor, relative, or associate, we need to be aware that everything is not just as "we" see it. Given the same circumstances, Joe Schmoe or Jane Doe may perceive the scene in a whole new light, a light that you didn't even know existed!

When two human beings cannot effectually communicate, there is a certain emotional perplexity that comes from not knowing what is going on in the mind of somebody else. It can be very strength-sapping as we try to guess if it was something we said or failed to do which caused the other person to become upset or distant, wondering what their next move will now be. The differences in the sexes were not created to cause turmoil, but to set us apart as unique individuals that must rely on the gifts of others. Neither sex is better than the other, but, together, both male and female serve their purpose here on earth.

The next time you get in to a tiff with loved one or associate, remember these differences, and perhaps then, you will be a little more understanding, sensitive, and patient. Learn to loosen up, laugh at, appreciate, and smile at our differences, and I guarantee your load will become a whole lot lighter!

While men and women may sometimes have difficulty communicating, our heavenly Father assures us, that those who call on Him will be answered! *"Ask and it will be given to you; seek and you will find; knock and the door will be opened."* -Matthew 7:7

How Does Your Garden Grow?

As a young child, upon my bedroom wall hung a poem stating, "The only way to have a friend is to be one." I'm certain I must have read that verse dozens, if not hundreds of times while laying upon my bed, and yet, it's simple but profound message continued to grow in my heart throughout my adult life. Whether it's friendship, marriage, or another form of loving relations, all relationships entail a foundation built on the acts of giving and receiving. As flowers soak up the rays of the sun, and droplets of dew, offering to man their fragrant and bright blooms, so too does every loving relationship require the loving gestures of both individuals.

How does *your* garden grow?

For five years, Tom had his eye on Sandra, a peppy and pleasant young lady who worked in his office. In the past, when Tom's schedule wasn't as demanding, Tom and Sandra shared lunches and spoke to each other often. Tom promised Sandra many a time he would take her out on a "proper date," but as the weeks, then months began to fly by and Tom's schedule became more hectic, Sandra gave up hope. In Sandra's mind, Tom was disinterested, so there was no sense in hoping for something that would never happen.

♥ SON Salutations

A year later, Sandra announced to her fellow employees that she was engaged to be married! When Tom heard the news, he was so shocked he turned white and had to sit down. "How can she do that to me? She should be marrying me, not him," whimpered Tom as a tear fell down his eye.

In that same office building, was employed a middle-aged woman named Helen, who was a divorced mother of a thirteen year old boy. As Helen sipped her coffee at her desk, she reflected on the messy argument she and her son had just before work. This was not their first fight, but the result of years of lack of communication and neglect. The truth of the matter was that Helen's son never knew for certain if his mother loved him or not, and this caused much conflict in their relationship.

The wealthy, elderly owner of the above mentioned building, Mrs. Emily Hawkins, was on her death bed in the hospital. The doctor notified her immediate family and friends, knowing they would want to say their final good-byes. All of Mrs. Hawkins children came, shedding heartfelt tears, but there were no friends to come because the wealthy Mrs. Hawkins never took the time to nurture meaningful friendships.

Real Life Application: What these three stories have in common is all their outcomes could have come out very differently if only they would have watered their gardens more carefully. Loving words unspoken, caring gestures never accomplished, time never given; all of these resulted in seeds of friendship and love being choked by bitter weeds of neglect, selfishness, fear, and all things which destroy, rather than build up.

How does your own garden grow?

Is there a special one, two or three flowers you wish to see blossom, and yet it never seems to grow? Then ask yourself how well you are caring for that tender bud. Is it being watered with kindness and thoughtfulness? Is the warmth of love freely administered as does the sun offer it's rays of light? Are the leaves of the flower pruned and nurtured continually with the gifts of time, energy, and self?

As I again ponder that verse which sat upon my wall for so many years of my childhood, it is my hope that, for those people who I "say" I love, be they spouse, children, or friend, that I will do my best to let my love, not be mere lip service, but to let the true heartfelt emotions which fill my heart, overflow and pour out, so that every blossom may be watered and never wither. In like manner, may the reality of God pour out into your own lives, so that your hearts can fully comprehend what is the height, breath, and width of His love.

Out of Evil

The temptations, even the rough spots along our journey of life, can be used for great good; if only we humble our self enough to look at what lessons we can learn from the trials we face.

Martha was an elderly woman who had completely let herself go. At one time, Martha was meticulous about her house-cleaning and personal appearance, but to see her now, one would think she were homeless, with no access to a hair brush or bath tub. From outer appearance, one may judge Martha as simply a woman who was lazy and sloppy, but only those closest to her knew of how the death of her husband of fifty years had caused Martha to plunge into the depths of grief and depression. The trauma of the sudden passing of her spouse forced Martha to also ponder her own death.

Martha's reaction to the natural cycle of life and death, was to hide and surrender, rather than grab hold of the time she had remaining, reaping the most joy before her time would too come.

Down the street from Martha, lived Harold and Kathy. At Harold's place of business worked a new unmarried secretary. It was not long before Harold and his secretary began having an affair. To those who knew of the not very well-hidden affair, Harold was marked as a playboy, but the reality of the situation was that Harold's affair was proof of the genuine status of his marriage.

Kathy, Harold's wife, never really loved Harold, but married him for selfish financial gain. So too, was Harold never truly in-love with Kathy, but was awed by her great shape and pleasant attitude which Harold knew would be a plus when he introduced his wife to the big-wigs at his office.

The marriage succeeded for a while, even producing Harold, Jr., but the truth of the situation could not be hidden forever.

One block over from Harold, lived Joan. Joan suffered from severe insomnia, and when she finally did manage to sleep, her rest was disturbed with terrible nightmares. While Joan's doctor simply handed her a prescription for sleeping pills, what would have helped Joan more would be to look at what was bothering her life so much that it would invade even her sleep. The truth of the matter was that Joan was living a very immoral life, and deep in her heart, she knew her spiritual welfare was at stake. This caused great fear and stress within Joan, thus, her insomnia and nightmares.

In all of the above stories we can see that if we dig beyond the surface, we will see that those things which cause conflict in our life, are often issues that have never been fully addressed. Temptation and inner turmoil, while an evil, can thus be used to help us understand ourselves, our weaknesses, and facets of our lives that need our positive care and attention.

Rather than succumb to sin, let us positively use turmoil as a magnifying glass which clearly reveals to us just how much we need Christ in our life.

A Second Chance at Love

While at a recent church bazaar, I had the opportunity to speak to many I normally don't have the chance to speak to in-depth at Sunday services. Sundays are a nice day to nod, smile, and offer a few moments of small talk before and after services, but the fellowship of the bazaar offered our church not only a chance to make some money, but gave members a lovely afternoon of conversation and laughter.

One particular couple I had seen often, assuming them to have been married for a long time, surprised me by telling me the story of how they met. Upon hearing the story, I was deeply touched because it was proof of how miraculously God CAN and DOES work in the lives of those who believe in Him!

When "Raymond" and "Bonnie" met several years ago, Raymond was a widower, and Bonnie was a widow. While I don't know every detail, it seemed obvious that God graciously and mercifully offered both Raymond and Bonnie a second chance at love.

As I heard the story of their meeting unravel before me, I was flooded with thoughts of how complex this tale really was.

Imagine for a moment, that the spouse you

have known and loved for what feels like a lifetime, has become critically ill, soon to find rest in the comforting arms of the Lord. Imagine the grief and shock one in this position must feel; the stabbing pain of one's heart being emotionally torn in two. For me, the pain is incomprehensible, and I admire anyone who can come out of the grief with sanity intact. And yet, the trauma of losing a loved one is only part of the package, for once the pain, shock and anger subside, and the reality of this profound loss makes its way to the surface, then one must learn how to face life alone.

Alone.

While the word alone does not necessarily have to also mean "lonely," many people who find themselves alone, tend to also find themselves feeling lonely. I believe it was said by Mother Theresa that, to be lonely is perhaps the worst sadness.

Loneliness is a profound feeling of facing the world alone, and there is no one to share in the laughter, joys, pleasures, and tears. As was the first man Adam alone, and God saw that it was not good for him, and created woman, so too is it better for man to not be an island unto himself. I can only imagine, that God, in all His kindness, reached down in to the lives of Raymond and Bonnie and, for whatever reason, bestowed upon them the greatest gift of all; the gift of love.

While most people only experience true love once, our heavenly Father presented to this loving couple a double portion of His very essence; love!

I watched that day, as the mature and womanly Bonnie sat upon Raymond's lap like a youthful, smitten schoolgirl. In their eyes were no longer signs of pain, but happiness and love. Only God could be so good.

Justifying Wrongdoing

Listen to someone who has been caught in an act of wrongdoing. Chances are that person will attempt to justify their wrongdoing, hoping that if there is a palatable motive behind their less than godly act, the wrong will somehow seem less bitter.

Just as Satan deceived Eve by telling her a lie, so too must we be cautious not to believe the lies we tell ourselves in order to make sin sweeter to our own soul.

Let us look at the following examples.

A husband commits adultery. When his wife finds out, he does not take full responsibility of his sinful action, but instead, attempts to justify sin by placing a large portion of the blame on his wife. "Well, if you showed me more affection, then I wouldn't have had to go looking for it elsewhere," he might insist. In another scenario, a boyfriend hits his girlfriend, issuing her a black eye. The following day, he cooks her breakfast, buys flowers, and blames his lack of control on her, stating, "I'm sorry for losing control, but you should know it makes me insanely jealous when you talk to other guys. If you wouldn't have gotten me so angry, this wouldn't have happened."

In this last situation, a woman on her way home from a stressful day at the office is cut off by another car. The woman has such a volatile bout of road rage that she reaches in to her purse, and using a small pistol she carries for safety, shoots at the offending driver while screaming at him hysterically. Thankfully, no one is hurt. While in court, the woman tells the judge, "I didn't mean to overreact, but I felt he was driving unsafely and was a risk to my life. Had he not cut me off, I would not have lost my temper in this terrible way."

All of these cases consist of individuals who refuse to be accountable for their own actions. Pride, selfishness, and spiritual blindness has allowed these individuals to not see the WHOLE picture, but only a small portion of the picture, which often selfishly and pridefully tends to be very self-serving.

Why is it so difficult for us to admit we may have been wrong, or there may have been a better way of handling a situation? Are we so prideful that that we have claimed godlike status? Will God love us less if He knows we may have erred?

No one, but God, is perfect, and that is why

♥ SON Salutations

God sent His Son to die on the cross for our sins. God, in all His loving kindness, knew that man was an imperfect being, and it is only through our ardent pursuit of righteousness that we may be saved. However, how can man pursue righteousness if he is blind and unwilling to open his eyes to his own unrighteousness? Unless we open our eyes fully to see the whole picture, not just the small parts that pertain to us, and then half the truth is still not truth. Had the woman in the last scenario been fully honest, she would have admitted to herself that although her fear over what she felt was a man who unsafely cut her off the road, was justified, how she reacted to that reality was not just, and in fact, was wrong. Had she also been brutally honest with her self, she would have also admitted her own unsafe excess speed, as well as a history of a volatile temper that often causes her to overreact. And finally, had this woman truly sought truth and righteousness in this case, she would have admitted her own dangerous act of shooting at another driver, offering him a sincere apology for handling the situation in such a poor fashion.

How easy it is to see the flaws in others, but do we have the courage to point this same critical finger at our self, inspecting all corners of our life?

When Christ hung upon the cross stripped of all his clothes, he allowed himself to made vulnerable as he took the stings of the crown of thorns, the lashings, the dagger to his side, and piercing to his flesh from nails. While Christ was guilty of no sin, yet allowed him self to take on the weight of sin so that we might have life, isn't the least we can do in honor and gratitude of this sacrifice is being accountable for our own wrongdoing?

Vision

The Creator made man with a brain. Within the complex workings of this intricate network of nerve endings and cellular matter exists the ability to ponder and dream, as well as serves as the home to our most deep emotions and recollections.

The brain is a fascinating instrument, and while it's intended purpose is for good, sometimes, unrealistic, obsessive, or negative thought patterns steer an individual farther away from God and goodness, rather than bringing him closer.

Dreaming dreams while a person is sleeping is one thing, and dreaming of positive opportunities and possibilities while awake is another, yet there is a difference between constructive dreaming and unrealistic fantasizing.

Fantasies may make me "feel nice" when I indulge in them, but do nothing to change my life in any godly way. In fact, unrealistic fantasies can make the individual so desire something that will, chances are, never be tangible, thus, desire turns in to obsessive, unhealthy hunger that can never be quenched.

Vision, on the other hand, is something entirely different.

Imagine what the world would be like if we all lay aside fantasies so that we may then embrace visions.

What is the burning vision you live for?

Vision is not just some quaint, sentimental idea of what we'd "like to have." We have to fan the vision into flame until it becomes like a glowing ember within us. Having a clear and godly vision opens up many more doors of possibility because, with God, all things are possible!

God cannot bless sin, but He CAN bless the life of the individual who seeks Him as diligently as the riches of the world!

The Gift of Self

"The only gift is a portion of thyself." - Emerson

As a very young child, I recall watching a children's film titled, "The Little Drummer Boy." The animated fictional story told about a poor shepherd boy who went to visit the Christ child on the day of his birth. When he arrived, the boy realized that other visitors presented the baby Jesus and his parents with gifts of gold, frankincense, and myrrh, but the shepherd boy had no gift due to his impoverished state. The only possession in the world the child had was a small handmade drum, and so, the little drummer boy gave the only gift he could give out of the pureness of his heart. The young shepherd picked up his drum, and as he looked in wonder at the Christ child, he played the best song ever; a drum solo inspired by the opening of his own heart.

Even as an adult, this animated cartoon never fails to bring a tear to my eye. Certainly, it is only a make-believe story, but the message it conveys is not only very real, but of great importance.

The gift of self is a most precious gift, indeed, because it is not a gift that can be purchased easily with money, but requires the time, energy, and heartfelt sentiments of the giver. For example, every mother knows how her heart leaps when her child presents her with a hand-drawn card, offers her a hand-picked flower, or gives her that old kindergarten standby, the noodle necklace! I don't know about you, but that silly noodle necklace was more precious to me than diamonds or pearls! This, my friends, is a gift of love. A gift of self.

There are birthday gifts, and Christmas gifts. Gifts of fruit, chocolates and flowers. However, the most precious gift known to all of mankind, is the gift of salvation our heavenly Father presented all of us when He allowed His Son, Jesus Christ, to be a living sacrifice for our sins. Our Creator did not "have" to do this, but He loved us so richly as individuals, that He gave to us the greatest gift He could give. The gift of love. The gift of self.

Don't Forget To Flush

At the risk of making you blush since I would dare use a "bathroom analogy," I'd like you to consider for a moment, your inner body as a vessel of sorts. Within this holding tank composed of flesh, blood, organs, bones, and nerves, often exists something else we didn't bargain for. In fact, one might compare this "substance" to the same sort of yucky build up that creeps in to the rim of our toilets, thus making a good, stiff cleaning brush and cleanser a welcome friend. As far as I know, this substance doesn't have a name, most likely because it is invisible to the naked eye. However, as does the microscope reveal bacteria and germs upon a toilet, so, too, does this unseen substance leave it's telltale signs in the form of emotional and spiritual distress. How this unwanted visitor enters our body's system is by neglecting to "flush" on a regular basis. Flushing doubt, fear, worry, negative and unproductive thoughts and emotions from our bodies on a daily basis is imperative if we are to function at optimal physical, mental, and spiritual levels. But, if we neglect to flush, it is not long before hidden resentments and negative thought patterns begin to subtly weaken our characters, self-esteem, outlook on life, and even affect our walk with the Lord.

We may attempt to cover up the bad smell of such festering emotions, but not even a strong deodorizer can mask the scent of a wounded and infected soul.

Not too long ago, I had to come face to face with this same reality in my own life. Due to the fact I had been a Christian for as long as I can remember, pride and ignorance caused me to be unaware of how I had certain un-addressed issues in my life, even as far back as childhood, that had been worn around my neck like a heavy chain. It was not too difficult to go about life carrying a few heavy links, but as my life progressed, and there would be another serious stress or strain, so too, would my "necklace of iron" gain a new link. It was only until the day I realized I was so weighted down with emotional baggage that I was not even able to effectually operate as a Christian, that I fully realized the importance of regularly "flushing" your inner "tank." For those next few weeks, I thus began a total elimination process; facing and addressing the many issues from my past that I had never fully laid to rest. I began to forgive those people involved who needed forgiving; no longer allowing resentment and scorn to abide inside me. Of the situations I could not control, I also laid worry and fear aside, instead opting to invite in peace and acceptance.

♥ SON Salutations

I have heard individuals who, upon pouring out their heart to another, refer to the outpouring as "cathartic." This is exactly what we must do each and every day, several times a day, if necessary, to ensure no impure or unproductive emotion or thoughts will find a home within us. Every day we must not only flush out those things that pull us farther away from God, rather than pull us closer to Him, but we must also do what we can to not even entertain such negative thoughts and emotions. Stressing, fearing, or obsessing over an issue will not make the issue go away, nor will these heal it.

There is only one true Healer, and He alone, is the source of peace, comfort, and joy.

Today, set your worries aside, and let them rest in the hands of God.

Judge Rightly

Have you heard the saying, "Don't judge a book by its cover?" This story is not only about wrongful judging based on outer appearance, but assuming one knows the contents of a book even before it is opened.

Tim was a quiet and gentle man who was never much interested in sports, but rather the finer things in classical music, fine art, antiques, and gourmet cooking. All through his life, Tim faced harsh criticism, even mockery, from peers who did not understand his interests. He even endured the inaccurate label of "homosexual" simply because he did not fit neatly into the common description of what a man "should" be. Once married and with children, the inaccurate judging did not end, but had now quieted down to a whisper; muffled comments uttered behind his back. Thankfully, although the unkind comments stung Tim now and then, he went on to be a very successful and admired professional in his field.

While Tim's story ended on a happier note, how many other people go on to be negatively affected by inaccurate or unkind criticism, giving in to and believing the labels they are tagged under?

♥ SON Salutations

As a much younger woman, I was introduced to a man whose massive arms were covered with tattoos. This bear of a man rode a motorcycle, wore leather, boots and the usual biker attire. Admittedly, I had misjudged this man, as had numerous others who feared him, and it was only until I took the time to know this man that I found out he was not only intelligent, respectful, and kind, but was someone I would be proud to call friend. From that point on, I was not so quick to judge a book by its cover.

Wrongly judging someone on physical appearance alone is one thing, but what about our occasional attempts to play God by reading an individual's attitude all wrong? How often do we see a person sitting alone while in a crowded room and think they are lonely or shy? Or worse, that he is anti-social or stuck-up. The truth of the matter could be this person is very confident, intelligent, and content simply observing others before he leaps into a conversation.

Our heavenly Father gave us a brain so that we may use it, thus, our ability to judge others is not wrong or ungodly, but, it is our Lord's intention that we judge fairly and righteously. If we wish God to be patient with us, then let us also be patient with others.

Musings On Mid-life

Lately, I've been thinking about aging. While my so-called mid-life crisis of nearing, then turning forty years old is long over, thank God, I am yet again pondering the issue of age, more specifically, accomplishing all I want to accomplish before I get too old. My biggest concern is that I will wake up one day and find out I have serious regrets; issues that could have been easily resolved when I was more physically and mentally able.

The other night, I thought of my life; where it has been and where it is going. It was not so long ago that I was a teen, thinking these same thoughts, the only difference was, the future held so much more time. It seemed more acceptable to procrastinate as a much younger woman because I knew I had so many more years before me.

Now, here I am, forty years old, and suddenly, time does not seem like such a gracious commodity. I find myself thinking of seizing time, rather than letting it slowly wash over me as so many people do.

Ancient Eastern philosophy suggests that age forty is a time of wisdom. Imagine that! Here I was dreading turning forty for the last few

♥ SON Salutations

years, and according to the Eastern ancients, I am not "over the hill," but at the prime of my wisdom!

In the Bible, we are told to search for wisdom as fervently as we would the riches of the world. How often do we do just the opposite, and search for earthly riches, while neglecting the most precious; spiritual wisdom? Perhaps, this mid-life reality check is God's way of reminding us what is truly important in life, because, although our bodies may begin to show signs of wear and tear, we can rejoice in the fact our souls will gain no wrinkles, no shades of gray, or loss of firmness. Like a fine wine that improves with age, we have the potential to reach higher and improved states of spiritual and emotional health, becoming more the inner beauties God would have us be!

I do not fear death, but I do fear not reaching my potential. There is nothing I can do to control getting older, but I **CAN** control **HOW** I will use the remainder of my time on this earth, and it is my vow to use it wisely.

Recently, a friend questioned me about a particular facet of my spiritual walk. I concluded that life would seem very shallow if I had no spiritual purpose. For me, a life without God, would be an existence similar to that of an animal. I would eat, sleep, and partake of a few bodily pleasures, only to one day die and wither away. What a tragedy this would be, yet how many people live exactly such a life, not knowing the goodness of God? When all is said and done, it is not really aging we dread, but not living life to the fullest.

If we are to reach our greatest potentials, then we must never turn our back on our spiritual essence, nor on its creator, God.

New Life

Keeping Watch

"No man knows how bad he is until he has tried to be good. There is a silly idea that good people don't know what temptation means." -C. S. Lewis

I have heard some new converts to Christianity state they couldn't wait to further grow in the faith so that they would be spared temptation to sin. I suppose that in their innocence, these individuals assumed a deeper level of godliness was akin to being on some sort of radiant pedestal whose walls are so high that not even sin can permeate them. Just pick up a newspaper or ponder certain past media events, and you will see that no man, not even the most vocal televangelists or small town preachers, priests or Christian lay people are spared from the snares of evil. In fact, quite the opposite is true, and the reason for this is simple. Satan has no need to bother those unbelievers he already has in his possession. So who does he seek to tempt most? Those who have committed their lives to righteousness!

In the Bible, we are told how Satan tried to tempt Christ while in the desert fasting. Here he was, the Son of God, and even HE was not spared the wicked taunts of the adversary! If it happened to Jesus Christ, it will also happen to anyone who would follow him.

The foundation of righteousness is level and straight, but the detour to Hell is filled with potholes, bumps and cliffs, thus, we must progress ever-vigilantly, doing the work of the Lord while also keeping watch of where we are stepping. When walking in a meadow of grazing cows, do we step in the piles of cow dung, or do we cautiously walk around them, avoiding any mess to our shoes?

The same is true with guarding what we expose our minds and eyes to. We may think that peering briefly at pornography, or lulling in seductive daydreams is no big deal, but there is no escaping the subtle harm such media play upon our inner being. Thinking patterns and how we relate to others can change, and the more we pollute our clean cistern with dirty waters, the more clouded our vessel becomes, until one day it is undrinkable. Thankfully, our heavenly Father, is quick to hear our cries of assistance during such times of temptation, and to toss us the life-preserver of His living word. However, it is up to us to take that first step toward preservation.

Alone we are nothing, but through Jesus Christ, all things are possible!

Gracious Giving

"We do not quite forgive a giver. The hand that feeds us is in danger of being bitten." - Emerson

As a much younger woman, I recall I had a hard time taking a compliment. Somehow, I had this notion it was a sign of conceit to just accept these well-meant affirmations. It was only until a friend became infuriated with my making excuses whenever I received a compliment, that I quickly learned to accept the true sentiment of the kind words spoken. Unfortunately, the lesson did not sink in as well as I thought, for as I grew older, and came to experience more of life's up's and down's, I began to sometimes grow suspicious of the gestures of other's. I thought perhaps they wanted something of me, rather than truly trying to give out of the sincere contents of their godly heart.

I am not alone in this occasional inability to simply accept the gift of the giver graciously, and without suspicion. Any one who has been betrayed by a friend or suffered unfair treatment at the hands of an associate or loved one, is less apt to handle good and godly giving gestures with the sentiment they are intended.

The same is often true with giving. Some times, our giving is stifled because we fear it will draw suspicion, rather than appreciation.

We are a people who tend to be very hard on ourselves. We look in the mirror and seek flaw before beauty, wondering how any one could ever find us appealing, be it from a physical, intellectual, or spiritual standpoint. Those who dare to offer a thoughtful word are often looked upon as having some selfish and hidden motive, for, we think, "How can they simply want to give me something JUST for the sake of blessing me?"

We often don't feel worthy enough to accept truths about our self, most likely, because we, ourselves, do not recognize the good in us. How can we love others if we cannot even love ourselves?

In the Bible, we are told the story of how Mary Magdalene washed the feet of Jesus, soothing them then with oil, and wiping them dry with her hair. Our Lord's reaction could have been, "Get away, silly woman! That is not appropriate!" Instead, our Lord accepted the gift, knowing that Mary's intention was to simply soothe the tired feet of her friend who had been walking on the dry, dusty ground for many days.

♥ SON Salutations

While we are thinking of giving and receiving good gifts today, let us also not forgot the most important gift of all, which our Heavenly Father bestowed upon all of mankind. It is the jewel of salvation which is freely set before each of us.

The JOY of the LORD is my strength!

Why?

Why do good people sometimes do inconceivably stupid things? I have asked my self this question for as long as I can remember, and still, I have no intelligent answer, other than blaming such things on the frailty human nature.

I can look back at the mistakes of my past and be astounded at some hideously foolish acts and irresponsible behaviors. "How could I have done such a thing?" I wondered, "That was so unlike me; so against my usual character." I can only say, thank God He is a merciful God.

The times in my life my behavior was no example of godliness in action, I regarded my unrighteous behavior almost as a form of insanity. Why? Because I was not in my right mind. For whatever reason, my judgment was blurred by pride, selfishness, or a lack of yielding to what I believe. Typically, my "right" mind would be kind, thoughtful, and loving, but this "other mind" was not so kind, nor was it the type of mind I would be proud to display before heaven.

In periods of overwhelming stress, this mind was quicker to frustration and anger. This other mind also seemed to allow my mouth to spew hurtful words, and permit me to act before thinking. Although I have tried to understand and find some rational reason for any less than suitable behaviors in my past, when all is said and done, some things are simply beyond human comprehension.

Recently, several acts of terrorism caused staggering destruction and loss of life in the United States. These malicious attacks were not directed solely to military personnel, but toward innocent and unsuspecting men, women, and children who were simply going about their everyday life. I searched for some just reason for these extreme acts of violence and destruction, and again, it was beyond human understanding. Insanity.

It is during these lapses in understanding, our only solution is to draw nearer to God, cleaving tight to faith. The tragedies the United States has endured, both presently and in the past - even painful events within our own personal lives -can either make us stronger, or we can allow them to make us crumble. Just as there is nothing we can do to replace the lives of the innocent victims of terrorism and war, so we cannot turn back the hands of time regarding our own past sins.

It has taken me many years to learn to lay my problems in the loving and all-encompassing hands of God, telling Him, "This matter is too heavy for me to bear, and too great for me to fully understand." By yielding to righteousness, rather than giving in to evil and allowing it to consume us, we will no longer be a victim or slave to sin.

Immediately after the recent acts of terrorism against the United States, we began to see an outpouring of love and compassion, not to mention a renewed sense of patriotism. Upon the blood of the injured and dead is now injected the life-giving blood of volunteers who stand in line for hours to assist others in need. Upon the crumbled and mangled buildings, doors have opened, offering food, clothing, and shelter to those who require it. In our churches and homes, prayers are being offered, and many families are holding their children tighter.

Evil, sin, and hatred will not reign when the people hold tight to God. There is victory in righteousness.

Elusive Butterfly

Long ago, in the land of Heart, lived a fair maiden who dared to dream dreams. As a young child, she recalled how her father would set her on his strong knee and tell her many wondrous stories about far away and exciting places; lands she somehow knew she would one day come to also travel upon. Of the many tales her father would tell, there was one particular story that always held special meaning, even carrying her into adulthood. It was the presumed true tale of a certain species of butterfly, one that was seen by very few. What made the butterfly highly sought after was its emerald green wings which housed two small heart shapes, one on each wing, thus its coined name, "the elusive butterfly of love." It was said that the person who finds the elusive butterfly would live happily ever after, thus, it is no wonder the maiden searched ardently for the rare insect.

As a child, the fair maiden would prance about the woods with a butterfly net; laughing, smiling, and dancing about in glee, certain she would soon catch the elusive butterfly, but, to no avail. Weeks turned into months, and months into years, and the fair maiden grew older and wiser, wondering if perhaps the elusive butterfly of love was just a silly tale that old fishermen pass on as they sip their bottles of whiskey at sea.

One day, tired of searching, the maiden set down her net, and placing her face in her hands she began to cry. Upon the drying of her salty tears, the fair maiden decided to go on with living, no longer would the search for the elusive butterfly be part of her life.

Life, indeed, did go on, and one day, when the fair maiden was going about her daily errands, an odd-looking shape fluttered about her head. The maiden waved her arms to shoo the insect away, but no matter what she did, it would keep flying about. The next day, the maiden was surprised to see the odd-looking shape back again. Closer inspection revealed it was some sort of moth or butterfly. In no way did it look like the elusive butterfly of love, in fact, this butterfly's markings and colors were quite different. And so, the fair maiden would go about her errands, and the odd-looking butterfly would follow her, returning each day to flutter about her head. It was not long before the fair maiden and the butterfly formed a unique relationship.

For some odd reason, the butterfly seemed to enjoy the maiden's company, and the fair maiden felt a sense of peace and comfort, knowing her winged companion would never leave her side.

Many years passed, and one day, for some strange reason, the fair maiden recalled how she used to search for the elusive butterfly of love. In fact, the more she looked at her faithful winged companion, the more she wondered about the validity of the story of the elusive butterfly. Curiosity soon began to turn into discontentment with the butterfly she had devoted so much of her life to. "Look at you," she whispered to her faithful companion as he sat upon her finger, "You are not beautiful emerald green. Now, especially after so many years, your wings are dull and frayed. Do not worry though, my little friend, you are not the elusive butterfly of love, but you have been faithful, good, and true. I will keep you by my side always."
The maiden set down her winged companion and went outside to the rose garden to get a breath of fresh air, and what did she see? Green as a sparkling cut emerald fluttering about, a pink heart on each wing; the elusive butterfly of love! Like a young school girl, the maiden pranced with glee, scarcely able to believe her eyes! Suddenly, it dawned on the maiden that now she must decide what to do; should she run for a net, or just watch the elusive butterfly as it flutters about her garden,

soon to fly away and most likely never be seen again. Joy turned to sadness as the maiden knew what she must do. The maiden gave the elusive butterfly one final look, acknowledging his existence, and turning away, walked out of the garden to return to her faithful winged companion who had befriended her so many years ago.

Inside the house, the maiden was shocked to see her dear friend looking strangely ill. His wings beat weakly, and he could not even manage to fly. The maiden gently picked up her companion and caressed him in the palm of her hand, clearly evident he was at the end of his life. Upon the butterfly's final breath, the maiden shed many tears, tears which flowed over her loving companions frail body. Suddenly, as if out of nowhere, a glimmer of light came from out of her hand. "What is this?" the maiden thought. The ragged wings of her beloved companion seemed to reveal under them something more lovely. Carefully, and tenderly, the maiden peeled away the tattered, old shell which encased her winged friends body, to reveal beautiful wings of emerald green, a small pink heart on each side. Both tears and joy filled the maiden's heart, and her story was thus passed down by old fishermen who sipped whiskey at the sea.

♥ SON Salutations

<u>Real life application</u>: Aren't we all guilty to some degree of searching for or desiring something that, in most cases, is right under our very noses? Thankfully, unlike the above fictional story, love is not elusive at all, and in fact, it is all around us, if we would only fearlessly trust, not only God, but the power of love.

Love Letters

I have a secret Love, who really isn't so secret at all. I think about Him often, speaking highly of Him in public whenever I have good opportunity. Sometimes people turn away and shake their heads, but His love runs so deep that I just want to run to the mountain tops and shout of how wondrous He is! He has been my Love since long ago, His devotion to me all these many years never ceases to leave me in awe. Even at my worst, He was there to hold my hand, and at my best, His blessings shower my life with joy! When others have uttered unkind words, or hit me with betrayal, He alone stood by my side; a pillar of strength, and a comforting pillow. Where human beings have failed, He alone has stood firm. His love is unchangeable. He is faithful, forgiving, merciful, and just, and despite these more gentle qualities, He is also powerful, knowledgeable and all-knowing!

His love for me is so rich and all-encompassing that I cannot imagine ever being without Him. I wouldn't want to be without Him, because a life without His love, would be a fleeting and meaningless existence.

When I first met my husband many years ago, I had to let him know that if I were to marry him, He would have to accept me knowing I would always put my other Love first; before husband, children, and all worldly possessions. Many years have passed and He is still a part of my family and my life. I know He will be there until the bitter end, and when I take my last breath, He alone will be there to carry me over the threshold between death and life.

I speak about God passionately because that is the type of relationship He calls us to have with Him. His undying love is not just for you or me, but for all who seek truth and righteousness. Indeed, He is our Creator and Heavenly Father, but His love is so rich that even in the Bible, His Son Jesus Christ, is regarded as the "husband," and the Church as His "bride." I have no doubt that it is God's desire for our relationship with Him to not only be fulfilling, but intimate. Secrets we might wish to tell a best friend, are best whispered into the attentive ear of our Heavenly Father, for unlike an earthly human, God's will is for our ultimate good.

Today, won't you join me in meeting the Love of your life?

Quarreling Over God

"But avoid foolish controversies and genealogies and arguments and quarrels about the law, because they are unprofitable and useless." -Titus 3:9

Some people waste a lot of time quarreling over God, and issues such as the theory of evolution, when was the world created, and what span in time was man formed. There is no doubt that God wants us to know His word and will, and to increase in wisdom and understanding, but how do we know when to speak, and when to let truth speak for itself? I can recall in my own family how my father-in-law and I used to love to get involved in a nice juicy debate every Christmas eve. He and my mother-in-law would visit from out of state, staying for a week or two in our home. When everyone else hopped in their beds for a good nights rest, my husband's father and I would settle in our living room chairs prepared to do battle; a match of wits in the heartiest of good spirits. Sometimes our discussions were about politics, and other times they centered around some popular controversial issue. My favorite however, was our late in to the night talks on God and the Bible. As much as I enjoyed these, however, there were some nights when I had to walk away from the discussion, not in defeat, mind you, but because there came a point in the debate when ego was getting in the way of truth, or true enlightenment was not being sought. My response in cases as this was always the same, "The truth does not need to be defended." I would then politely excuse myself, give my father-in-law a hug, and tell him how much I enjoyed our talk, and I would leave the rest in God's hands.

As my above story reveals, sometimes it is easy to get caught up in the heat of debate or quarreling, and truth becomes secondary. In cases as this, it is more important to be right, than to be lovingly working toward truth. There are also moments when Biblical quarreling can turn more in to a silly or viscous form of entertainment, and once again, the spirit of truth is forgotten. I have learned through my own experiences that while we are called to be messengers and sharers of the God's good news, that news becomes soured when it is used as hateful verbal daggers, or prideful spews rather than issued in the spirit of love and generosity. In short, verbal wars can be a deterrent from truth so it is best to simply let truth speak for itself all in God's good time. Sometimes, trust in God, and patience is the only way for truth to set its own course.

♥ SON Salutations

Heavenly Father, thank you for letting me be wise enough to know when to speak, and when to remain silent. Thank you for giving me the wisdom to know when it is best to embrace my enemies, rather than shun them. Grant me the ability to cleave to your word, rather than my own pride. This I ask in the name of your son, Jesus Christ. Amen.

Gentle Giant

"Someday love shall claim his own. Someday right ascend his throne. Some day hidden truth be known; some day, some sweet day." -Lewis J. Bates

Having heard nothing but good comments about a certain animated movie geared for both young and old alike, I went to the theater to see the film, "Shrek." In the movie, Shrek is an ornery, but lovable ogre, who, due to his large size and slightly freakish appearance, is feared by most people who cross his path. Although Shrek dreams of being loved by a fair maiden who would love him in turn, he knows that as reality has it, no woman in her right mind could or would ever love someone as hideous as him. And so, Shrek exists alone, accepting his lonely fate, until, by amazing circumstances, he comes to meet a beautiful princess.

I won't spoil the ending of the movie, but what drew my attention most about this movie was that the main character was not beautiful in the classical sense of the word, and yet he comes to reign triumphant, saving an entire village, fending off numerous enemies, and displaying more character and depth than most other "normal-looking" men. It is sad that poor Shrek has to endure name-calling and be looked upon with fear and scorn simply due to his different physical appearance. The sadder picture is that while this movie is pure fiction, within our own society such travesties do occur.

How often are we all guilty of prejudging someone based on appearance alone?
As the ogre, Shrek, suggests in the movie, we are more than what we appear on the outside, and inside this external shell lies many layers. The question is, will we take the time to peel the layers so that we may see all men for who they really are?

Just as we should look deeper than the surface of all human beings, so too, does God see into the core of our heart. While we may be able to deceive mankind, there is no hiding who we really are from the ever-watchful eye of our Creator.

How thankful we should be that God does not use our same overly-critical standards to deem our worthiness of His love.

A Time to Let Go

The Bible relays there is a season for all things. *"There is a time for everything, and a season for every activity under heaven: a time to be born and a time to die, a time to plant and a time to uproot, a time to kill and a time to heal, a time to tear down and a time to build, a time to weep and a time to laugh..."* (Ecclesiastes 3:1-4)

As a people who cherish life and all its joyous splendors, we often tend to overlook the inevitable tears and pains that also will be placed upon the road of life. How we perceive our hurts, and what we chose to do with them once they pass, is, however, all up to us. Will we allow pain and suffering to overcome us, or will we reign victorious, allowing life's stings to help us come to deeper levels of appreciation and understanding?

One particular author whose name I can't recall, wrote that without sadness we would not know happiness, and without darkness, we would not know light. The author's point is that obstacles we may encounter in life can work FOR, rather than AGAINST us, if we allow them to.

In my own life, when there was a death

amongst friends or relations, once the tears had dried, I allowed the death experience to teach me to better appreciate my own life, even loved ones. Thus, I was able to, not only reevaluate what was godly or ungodly in my life, but I learned to show my love better to those I truly loved. The same is true during periods I may come down with an illness. Once the sickness is over, I am just about ready to do handsprings over what a blessing it is to be healthy and whole again!

The same is true with falling into sinful paths. Either we can learn and grow from our mistakes of the past, or we can let them conquer and destroy us.

Just as there is a time to fight and a time to rest, so too, is there a time to let go of the often painful past. Not one of us is perfectly free from sin, nor are we spared from life's up's and down's, thus, let us use the merciful gift God has given us, and let us take advantage of His peace and forgiveness!

Flowering Forth

"A morning-glory at my window satisfies me more than the metaphysics of books." -Walt Whitman

Consider for a moment, a tulip bulb. Withered and brown, it holds deeply inside it a potential and beautiful new life. Miraculously, the seemingly unattractive round bulb can hold safely in its core a prized flower of pink, yellow, red or white, yet to look upon the odd-looking object in the palm of one's hand, who would know that within such a proverbial "ugly ducking" could exist such a brilliant "swan!"

Unlike the swan though, the bulb, if not properly nurtured with water, earth, and sunlight, will never begin the metamorphosis it is capable of! Instead, the bulb will just sit in a box or corner of someone's basement awaiting someone to come and plant it.

So too, does our Heavenly Father have a gift for us just waiting to be opened and brought forth to life! It is the gift of salvation! Unfortunately, like the untouched tulip bulb that sits on a ledge gathering dust, so too, do many people never come to know and experience the beautiful blooming forth of the spirit of God in their life! As the bulb needs sunlight and water to spring it to full existence, our spirit requires the nourishment of the truth of God and His word to permeate the hard, outer shell of sin that encases our hearts. By inviting Christ in to our life, we can be transformed from a spiritual bulb to a blooming sprout! The continual watering and nurturing of spirit will thus provide a lovely and colorful flower that reaches ever upward toward the radiant light of Christ, and its fragrance is indeed sweet!

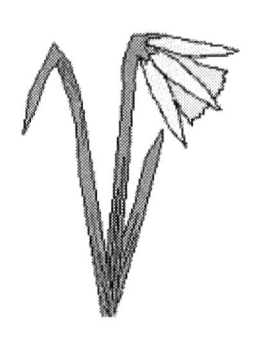

Right Things, Wrong Places

Upon entering her first year of college, Lindsey was surprised to see so many different types of people from all walks of life. What amazed her most however, were how peers who claimed to seek truth and goodness did so in paths which seemed far from honest or good.

Jamie, the slender and tall girl from New York, who was Lindsey's roommate, claimed to be a witch. "Oh, we don't practice evil, we just do good spells and worship nature," Jamie insisted, as she rubbed garlic all over her walls to ward off evil spirits.

Another student, Martin, was into trying to predict the future via tarot cards and the Ouija board. Every Saturday night at 10 pm, Martin and his friends would get together, drink beer, and share the secrets the deceased in the spirit world had revealed to them.

All of these people claimed to be seeking righteous truth, but Lindsey could not help but notice that these people did not seem any more happy or wise than she. Lindsey wondered, "Were these people looking for right things in all the wrong places?"

Lindsey's years in college clearly revealed to her a sad reality, yet how many of us today continue to have the best of intentions while seeking to fulfill our desires in all the wrong places?

One of the most abused desires is to be loved, yet how many people end up filling this very normal desire with ungodly substitutes as the misuse of sexual relations, abusive relationships, and various other media that do nothing to promote or support healthy love?

If we can so easily fall into detours that pull us farther away from our goals, then it is definitely worth looking into how we are filling our search for the spiritual, namely, God. For if these media having to do with mind and body can be abused, then the potential for spiritual abuse is present as well.

In the Bible, Jesus is quoted, *"I am the way and the truth and the life. No one comes to the Father except through me."* (John 14:6) We are also told, *"Then you will know the truth, and the truth will set you free."* (John 8:32)

If truth is supposed to make us free, then why are so many people in such bondage? Why do they lack peace, purpose, joy? The only natural conclusion is they have looked for truth in all the wrong places.

We cannot fill spiritual voids with worldly wisdom and we cannot find God in a pit of vipers.

Temptation

John A. Shedd, author of "Salt from My Attic," had this to say about temptation," *Many men have too much will power. It's won't power they lack.*"

This sentiment of not giving in to one's desires seems to go against what society tends to support; the idea that man should not deprive himself of everything he craves. Want a burger and fries even though the doctor said your cholesterol was too high? Go and get it at the local fast food restaurant!

Getting tired of your spouse? Divorce them and find a new one!

Bored? Go out and have a fling!

Feeling down in the dumps? Let's get drunk and stoned! After all, everybody is doing it!

Not every urge, craving, and desire is a worthy one, for even the drug addict hungers for his next high, yet we all know drugs are bad for you!

Saying, "No," to temptations seems to not only go against the "Go for it" philosophy many people in our society promote, but even our body and mind seems to fight as we deprive it of the fuel it hungers for, regardless if this "fuel" is good or bad for our spiritual and emotional welfare.

Many people perceive temptation as a bad thing. The reality is that it is not a bad thing, but a human thing. Everyone has faced temptation of one form or another in their life. Temptation shows us where our weaknesses lie, and it is the wise man who uses this information to his best advantage. These weaknesses that become revealed to us through temptation are areas in our life which the devil knows he may find either an open door, or even a tiny crack he can slip into.

The good news is, the more we say, "no" to temptation and ungodly desires, the more we actually strengthen those weak spots! God does not desire us to run and hide from temptation, but to face it head-on so that we may clearly see the potential pit before us. God desires us to confess our sins, admit our weaknesses, and to ask Him for the strength and wisdom we need to stand against evil.

Today, thank God for loving you so much that He has allowed you to use temptation as a means of seeing, and thus overcoming, your sinfulness.

Right Acts, Wrong Reasons

Peter was a man who was not well-liked. Like the character of Scrooge, in the Charles Dickens classic, "A Christmas Carol," Peter's life held no such positive turnaround. He was a bitter man who never had a kind word for any one, was stingy and selfish. No one knows for certain why Peter began to soften and appear to have a change of heart, but those people he had hurt or touched in a negative way were glad to see some new shreds of civility and decency in Peter, who was now approaching his sixtieth year upon the face of the earth.

As word of Peter's more gentle attitude got out, people Peter had wronged began to approach him in hopes of some sort of apology or peace settlement. "Do you remember me?" asked one elderly gentleman, "My dog's barking irritated you so you threw a rock at our window." Peter looked the man in the face and replied, "Oh yes. That was unfortunate about your window. Here's fifty dollars to cover the cost of replacing it." Peter smiled wryly, tipped his hat and continued walking down the street.

Shortly after, a young girl approached him, "Sir, do you know me? You shoved me aside last week so you could pass me on the sidewalk. Look. I'm wearing the same torn dress," stated the young child who had a look of pity in her eyes. Reaching into his pocket, Peter handed the girl a twenty dollar bill, patted her on the head, and continued walking on until he came to his home.

The remainder of Peter's three years on earth was spent in much the same way. Peter was feeling some regret toward the wrongful actions of his past, and in his attempt to settle the score, especially as the end of his life was approaching, this was the only way he knew how. Poor Peter would never come to know the peace and mercy of our Lord Jesus Christ.

Real life application: Many people confuse repentance with regret. While regret is indeed a *part* of repentance, it does not come close to the biblical concept of the type of inner transformation true repentance entails. Regret means being sorry. It is easy to be sorry for the wrong reasons though. I may be sorry because my wrong deed resulted in unexpected consequences, rather like the child who gets spanked for purposely breaking a window, whose regret has more to do with the upcoming probable spanking than with any sense of the wrong he committed. Slightly more nobly, I may be sorry because of the hurt my behavior caused to somebody else.

It is right and proper to be sorry in such cases, but it still doesn't go far enough. True repentance means being sorry for our wrongful behavior for the right reasons, not because I got caught and punished, and not even primarily because innocent persons were hurt, but because it was simply wrong. Not because the results were wrong, but because the action itself was fundamentally wrong.

Being sorry, even for the right reasons, is by no means all there is to repentance. True repentance involves a complete change of heart about what happened, a complete renunciation of the sin. It means a commitment to make a complete break with what I did that was wrong; a resolution never to commit the same deed again. Repentance also means facing up to what we have done wrong and not trying to sugar-coat our own participation by blaming our sins on others. There is no such thing as repentance without facing our sin personally, honestly and squarely, and without making a sincere effort to make right with the person we have wronged or hurt, promising the Lord that if our paths ever cross, we'll do what we can to make things right.

The words, *"I'm sorry. I was wrong,"* can be like a gift of the finest gold. So, too, can we prove the contents of our heart by simply being living examples of our renewed spiritual transformation, being the barer of light, rather than darkness.

The character in the above story tried to remedy the wrongs he had committed. It was a noble effort in many ways, especially as compared to the life he had led earlier, for true repentance must include making reparations where possible. But his attempts centered on buying himself into the good graces of his victims.

Just as salvation cannot be bribed or bought, neither can true repentance.

a tree is known by its fruit

Logic vs. Miracles

Miracles do not produce faith, but faith produces miracles. This maxim goes against our human instinct.

The Scriptures tell us that many people demanded a sign to authenticate the authority of Jesus of Nazareth. They claimed that if only they could see such a sign, they would they believe in Him. He replied, *"A wicked and adulterous generation asks the LORD for a sign..."* (Matthew 16:4)

The same principle is true of logic. Logic does not precede revelation, but follows it.

When God works a miracle, we can usually put it into a fairly logical frame of reference after the fact, but we typically cannot ascertain the ways of God in advance using logic or any other mental faculty. *"...God has chosen the foolish things of the world to shame the wise, and God has chosen the weak things of the world to shame the things that are strong..."* -I Corinthians 1:27

The Bible is replete with examples of men whom God raised up, who were often not "qualified" for the tasks to which God called them. By faith and the hand of God, God's will was indeed done. Let us look at the example of these men.

When God called Moses to deliver his people, Moses was an old man of eighty years. His own people, whom he hardly knew, had rejected him a generation earlier, and he had spent the last forty years in the desert, tending sheep. He knew practically nothing about the conditions that his people currently faced, and the present generation of his people didn't even know that he existed. The levers of power, which might have been available to him in his younger years, were long since gone. A leader of the people ought to be an inspiring speaker, but Moses wasn't. An earthly employer would not have given Moses a second look, but our Heavenly Father saw the greater picture.

Another example is David. David was the youngest of seven sons. There was nothing distinguished about David's family line, and his own background as a shepherd was hardly suitable training for a king. Once again, we see that God's ways are not man's ways.

The final example is the Twelve Apostles. According to worldly standards, the only one of the twelve who had any of what the world would call acceptable qualifications was Judas

Iscariot. The other apostles were mostly uneducated fishermen, hardly the kind of people who could be expected to turn the world upside down. Their personal qualities were hardly more appealing. The Scriptures paint Peter as an abrasive and opinionated man. John and James had a major problem with their anger, and Matthew was a despised tax collector.

Jesus saw something in each of these men that nobody else saw. The Son of God was looking to the future and saw the apostles, not as they were, but as he knew His Father could make them. Jesus had insight into "the final product."

In all of the above examples, God gave no thought to outer appearance, quality of speech, or worldly importance. What matters to God is not the outer man, but the inner being; what lies in the heart. God knew the potential all these men had, as well as how they would come to thirst for truth and righteousness.

Logic and deduction will not reveal the ways of God to us because our Father's ways are of a heavenly and miraculous realm that knows no boundaries! Those things that are impossible to man are made possible through faith in God!

Character

This is what author David Marion had to say on character, *"It's not what you were, it's what you are today."*

No time period thus far has had the greatest technological and medical advances of this generation. Yet, despite these advances, man has taken many steps backward regarding character.

There was a time when a man's mere verbal statement was as honored and respected as an officially signed court document. Treaties were often made and lands bought and sold on the gold-bonded word of a gentleman. Dare to question or challenge a gentleman's word, and you would find yourself having deeply insulted this man.

Due to simple human frailty, all of us, at some time or another, are guilty of displaying character that is less than noble. In the end however, no one is hurt more by flawed character than God and ourselves. We can allow our word to crumble and let the trust others place in our hands be used to advance our own selfish purposes, but when all is said and done, it is we who must face our real character when we look in the mirror at the

♥ SON Salutations

end of the day.

Author, Dwight L. Moody, states, *"Character is what you are in the dark."*

Thomas was a man who dressed well, ate well, and spoke well. He was considered "the upper crust," and well-respected by his friends and relations. In the light of day, Thomas contributed to charities, tipped his hat to young ladies, and told the minister what a fine job he did on Sunday's sermon. Behind closed doors was another story, however. Once in the privacy of his home, Thomas was bitter and stingy. His wife feared him, and his children had no respect for such an emotionally cold father. In the light of day, Thomas put on a good show, but the truth of character seeps out when we think no one is watching.

Someone IS watching. God. Take a look in the mirror today. What do you see? If God were standing beside you, would your character be something to be proud of, or ashamed of?

The good news about character is that it can be changed! Do not be ashamed, but find honor in the fact you are ready to cast away the old, and put on the new!

If I Could Do Life Over Again

While in a deeply reflective mood, I asked myself, if I could do life over again, would I have changed anything? I have heard this question asked before, and in many cases, the individual answering claimed to be fairly content with the past, and thus, would not change anything.

Looking back on my own forty years, I cannot share this sentiment. Most regrets on my part do not concern activities I never had a chance or desire to do, such as bungee jumping or skydiving, but, more commonly focus on "attitude." For one thing, if I could do life over, I would be much more fearless, for fear has often held me back from reaching out and boldly making new friends. It's also prevented me from taking some godly risks which may have improved my life.

If I could have a new lease on life, I would also be less concerned about how others might perceive what I do or say. There are times I would have liked to have screamed out and run in the ocean surf, or to break into spontaneous song or dance, but did not.

If I could do life over again, I would appreciate more, taking my time to really stop and smell the roses. I'd spend more time enjoying family, friends, and even such simple pleasures as a warm cup of tea on a cold winter's day. If I could turn my life around, I would love more richly, utter more kind words, share more smiles, and offer more warm embraces.

As my list of regrets went on, admittedly, I felt my spirit begin to sink a bit. Just then, a small voice inside me said, "It is never to late to change! The past is past and tomorrow is a brand new day!"

How true that statement is! And isn't this what the concept of repentance is all about? We all have regrets and have made mistakes, but by inviting Christ into our lives, we can truly be released from the occasional hurtful bondage of the past. In so doing, we are made into new creatures by the cleansing of God's word! *"Therefore, if anyone is in Christ, he is a new creation; the old has gone, the new has come!"* -II Corinthians 5:17

Won't you join me today by becoming a new creation?

Reaching Out of Ourselves

"We know ourselves best when we love, and so, as personalities, we have expected our relationships - and usually a single relationship - to be a total experience of love." - Daphne R. Kingma

My grandparents are now deceased, but I always admired their individual characteristics, as well as how they adjusted these same qualities to make their marriage more pleasant. Grandpa was very interested in sports, especially football and baseball. Every so often, he would travel to New York City to see the New York Yankees and, after a few days of fun and frolic with "the guys," Grandpa would return feeling like a new man.

My grandfather was not a very talkative man, unless, of course, the topic was sports.

His wife was quite the opposite! Grandma could talk from morning until night if need be, thus, she deeply valued the many social groups she belonged to, as well as her numerous friends.

What I admired about this couple was that both Grandma and Grandpa accepted each other for who they were, rather than making each other feel guilty for who they were not. Instead of looking at Grandpa's lack of talkativeness as a flaw which could have driven a huge wedge in their marriage, Grandma accepted her spouse as the man he was, knowing that his lack of constant conversation was no true indication of the love they shared.

I have seen marriages crumble because, rather than compromise, husband and wife seemed more concerned with power struggles and getting their own way. The solution of acceptance and compromise my grandparents applied so successfully to their differences allowed an otherwise good marriage to be saved, rather than abandoned.

Love is indeed a very fulfilling emotion, but romantic relationships are not its only source. Love can also be found in friendship and in reaching out to others.

Mother Theresa had no earthly husband, yet she stated repeatedly that she felt very loved and content in her life, through reaching out in love to others and allowing their love to fill her.

There is another type of love that is so fulfilling and all encompassing that its radiance has been known to melt even the coldest of hearts. It is the love of God, our Father, and His son, Jesus Christ.

Won't you reach out to Him today?

Listen To The Wind

"Love silence, even in the mind; for thoughts are to that as words are to the body, troublesome: much speaking, as much thinking, spends. True silence is the rest of the mind; and it is to the spirit what sleep is to the body, nourishment and refreshment."
-William Penn

Have you ever found yourself not thinking one single thought; no worry or care to creep into your mind? For most people, these times of inner silence are few and far between, but when they do occur, they are a soothing balm to our soul.

Having recently relocated from a busy suburban town to a secluded rustic setting far from the beaten path, I find myself having more and more of these quiet moments. Most of these peaceful incidences have occurred right within our own yard, such times as early morning when I will find my self looking out our big picture window, just looking at the snow covered forest that blankets our new home. As the day progresses, I watch the birds and squirrels that feed from the bounty of the land and several times I have even seen deer as they cross our yard to get to a nearby stream.

♥ SON Salutations

I find myself at a slower pace these days, but it is in no way due to a lack of energy or loss of youth. The small moments of tranquility have played an important part in my well-being and it is comforting to know that all these gifts were brought about by the loving hand of God.

All around us are gifts, but we are often just too darn busy to notice.

When was the last time you stopped to smell a flower? When was the last time you felt the soft cheek of a child? When was the last time you turned off the TV and radio for the day and just enjoyed the sound of coffee perking or birds chirping? When was the last time you told your loved ones, "I love you?"

Just as we can greatly benefit from moments of peace and tranquility, there is something even more important we need; a relationship with our Creator, God.

While our physical and emotional well-being will smile upon the peace we give it, so, too, will our spirits rejoice when we feed it the living word of God!

Putting Boundaries on God

As a young girl, part of my grade school education included attending mass several times a week. Since I was taught from a young age to place all my cares in the hands of the Lord, I innocently laid in my Father's hands an issue that was troublesome to me, my desire to straighten my terribly crooked teeth. After years of praying that same daily prayer, my parents finally had paid off my eldest sister's braces, and were now ready to consider the added expense of my own! "Praise God," I thought, "My prayer has been answered!"

Some may call it sheer coincidence, and others may even balk at the idea of daring to ask God for something dealing with a nature other than the spiritual realm, but I simply don't think it is spiritually healthy to restrict and place boundaries upon our intimacy with GOD. I believe we are to take Him into confidence on ALL matters, great and small.

Is God some kind of Spartan general who desires to ration out only what you "need"? Or is He a loving Father who longs to lavish good gifts on his children?

If you're a parent, ask yourself, How would you feel if your kids asked you only for what they "needed?" Wouldn't that break your heart? Surely you desire them to be intimate with you and tell you about all their hopes, fears and desires, however trivial they may be.

Do you suppose God desires anything less?

By putting boundaries around what kind of things you ask God for, you are missing out on a blessing that could be yours, as God deems fit. The fundamental issue is not to promote GREED, but of godly NEED: Our dependence on God, and developing a heart-to-heart intimate relationship with our Heavenly Father. By opening our entire lives to God, we are showing Our Creator that He is not only Lord of our complete life, but that we trust HIM and HIS judgment, resting our very lives in His loving and capable hands.

Cleave To The Cross

"But he was pierced for our transgressions, he was crushed for our iniquities; the punishment that brought us peace was upon him, and by his wounds we are healed. We all, like sheep, have gone astray, each of us has turned to his own way, and the LORD has laid on him the iniquity of us all." - Isaiah 53:5-6

The above Bible scripture begins and ends with Christ paying the price for our sins, but do you see what is sandwiched in the middle? A promise of healing!

God sacrificed His Son, Jesus Christ, so that you and I may be saved from the very sins Satan tries to condemn us with!

Have you recently made a decision to abandon sin and immorality, but are already beginning to lose focus on the salvation God has promised those who repent? Then direct your gaze to the cross! Fill your mind with that image of Christ paying the price so that we don't have to.

Healing comes not from dwelling on past sins and torturing yourself with guilt, but by allowing the love of God to soak through your heart and soul!

Regarding past repentance of sins, we are told in the Bible,"...*I will completely blot out the memory of Amalek from under heaven.*" -Exodus 17:14

When the Israelites came up out of Egypt, the Amalekites came against them with the sword. Just when God was starting to do something, Amalek (a figure of Satan) was there to try and undo what God was doing.

As you focus on the cross, some individuals may try and steal away your newfound salvation, but just as in times past, God promises that our steadfastness will not be in vain! *"Can plunder be taken from warriors, or captives rescued from the fierce? But this is what the LORD says : 'Yes, captives will be taken from warriors, and plunder retrieved from the fierce; I will contend with those who contend with you, and your children I will save.'"* -Isaiah 49:24-25

Notice the wording of the above Bible verse. Your marriage and your family are very precious to God, and He promises that if others persecute you due to your cleaving to the cross, God will deal justly with them.

We all have sinned. Only God is perfect. Whether you have already made a commitment to Christ, or are contemplating on doing so, no man will ever find salvation by remaining in sin. Sin will bind your neck like a noose, and sit upon your back as a heavy rock. There is no peace or joy in evil.

"When I kept silent, my bones wasted away through my groaning all day long. For day and night your hand was heavy upon me; my strength was sapped as in the heat of summer." Psalm 32:3-4

Today, won't you join me in cleaving to the cross? Alone we are weak, but with Christ, all things are possible!

The Gift of Friendship

*"Friendship is a priceless gift that cannot be bought or sold, but its value is far greater than a mountain made of gold - for gold is cold and lifeless, it can neither see nor hear, and in the time of trouble it is powerless to cheer.
It has no ears to listen, no heart to understand, it cannot bring you comfort or reach out a helping hand. So, when you ask God for a GIFT, be thankful if He sends not diamonds, pearls, or riches, but the love of real true friends." - Helen Steiner Rice*

I have been thinking a lot about friendships lately, due to what appears to be an abundant supply of quaint poems or stories sent to my email box by well-meaning friends and relations. For a while, my mail box was so continually full of such anecdotes, that, to be honest, I began to delete the messages without even reading them. Then, one day, as I was cleaning out my inbox, my gaze fell upon a certain poem which strangely caught my attention. The poem was about the value of friends. Upon inspecting the poem further, I began to feel a bit low, because I was guilty of doing exactly what this short story conveyed. I was taking friendship, even love, for granted. While someone had taken the time and energy to send me a poem that touched their heart in some small special way, I was tossing this gift by the wayside without even opening it.

Instead of being thankful and joyful that someone was thinking of ME at that moment, I twisted their good intentions into an inconvenience, thinking such thoughts as, "Don't they know how busy I am?" "Do they think I have nothing better to do than read poems all day?" A sense of shame fell over me and I vowed to appreciate my friends more.

True friendship is an expression of the soul. It is the outpouring of the gift of our self to another willing and open "vessel" known as "friend."

True friendship is also a form of love. It has taken me this long in life to realize this and I can only say I am grateful to have learned this truth before I leave this earth. If then, friendship is a form of love, isn't it wise that we treat our friends lovingly? Yet, how often are we guilty of not treating our friends and loved ones as the precious gems they are, but, instead, use when it's convenient for us, later pushing them aside once our own personal motives have been fulfilled?

Today, I propose that, if you have a friend you value, tell them! Unless you are willing to GIVE friendship, you cannot fully RECEIVE friendship! In like manner, we can only truly know love at its FULLEST, by knowing God, and inviting His Son, Jesus Christ, in to our heart and life.

Beautiful Trust

*"He has made everything beautiful in its time.
He has also set eternity in the hearts of men, yet
they cannot fathom what God has done
from beginning to end."* - Ecclesiastes 3:11

In all of our lives there are times when we must take risks and make leaps of faith. Whether it's trusting a job service to find you a suitable job now that you have just handed over to them all the money in your wallet, or the trust one places in a friend who promises us true friendship, we all take physical and emotional chances.

Spiritually, we take the biggest risks of all, because the choices we make today can affect the outcome of tomorrow.

I am always awed at how people can put so much faith in good luck charms, daily horoscopes, and other questionable mediums which tout spiritual nirvana, yet when it comes to placing faith in the hands of the One who created us, many individuals regard it as too risky a proposal. The same can also be said of those people who already believe in God, yet they are unwilling to let their faith take root and grow.

When God tells a person to walk forward, we should not ask, "What next? What will this step lead to? What will happen if I obey?" God may give us a glimpse into a different future, but we cannot fully fathom how the road we are following will ever get us there. Things happen in our lives, and we cannot see how such events fit into the picture at all. In God's timing, it will all become clear, but for now, we are only called to obey, trust, and have faith. One day, we will be able to look back and see that God did indeed make everything beautiful in its time, and we will be overjoyed at that which stemmed from trust.

Coincidence or God?

*"At first laying down, as a fact fundamental,
that nothing with God can be accidental."*
 -Longfellow

A friend and I were discussing miracles. It is interesting to note how some people, when faced with a miraculous situation, interpret the events as nothing more than pure coincidence. While events that result from pure chance may occur, it is an injustice to God to chalk up all miraculous events as such.

In my own life, especially as a younger, single woman, there were times that I needed a virtual miracle to pull me out of a desperate situation. When these prayers were answered, some of my friends rolled their eyes, insisting the only astounding thing to happen was that good luck had fallen my way. However, deep in my heart, I knew the miraculous truth. I had no tangible evidence to prove that God had His hand in these events. I'm certain that even if God did choose to offer me something tangible, such as a boulder crashing through my living room bearing the engraved inscription, "This is God," the doubters would still find some loophole through which to explain the amazing phenomenon.

♥ SON Salutations

This same friend then raised the issue of coincidence VS God's miraculous authorship in the Bible, specifically, the first book of the Bible, Genesis. He noted how the Messianic line always seemed to produce a surplus of sons, but few daughters. Nahor, (Abraham's brother), Ishmael, and Jacob had twelve sons each. We know that Ishmael had at least one daughter, (who married Esau), as did Jacob, but Nahor apparently had none. He did have one granddaughter, however, through his son Bethuel (see Genesis 22:20-21). It dawned on my friend that there could have been only one candidate who could fulfill the qualifications laid down by Abraham for a bride for his son Isaac, *"Go to my country and to my family, and take a wife for my son Isaac." (Genesis 24:4).* No wonder Abraham's servant asked, *"What if the woman is unwilling to follow me to this land?" (Genesis 24:5).*

He had only one chance to get it right! Everything that God had promised to Abraham, the entire Messianic line and the destiny of the world, hung on the agreement of one woman to walk away from her family, forsake and leave behind everything she knew, forgo the certainties of the settled city life for the dubious honor of becoming the wife of a nomad, an alien in a strange land without a square cubit of land to call home!

The amazing thing is that when the stakes are really high, God doesn't necessarily expand the options. On the contrary, He more often narrows them down to just one. That is not an accident, it is God's design.

Think of a time you may have been deeply lost in sin. At the point you realized you needed help, did your options expand or decrease? Based on my own experiences, my options decreased. There were only two choices: good or evil. Given my true heart and desire for righteousness, that choice became narrowed to one. The choices were to either reach for God, or remain entrenched in sin, something I wanted no part of.

There are no coincidences when it comes to spiritual matters. The only confusion lies in our understanding of God's abilities, which are boundless!

Greener Grass

"The grass isn't greener on the other side of the fence. It's greener where you water it more." - Anonymous

With the assistance of her grandfather, a young child planted a small garden of beans, peas, carrots, and radishes. The ground was tilled, seeds planted, and all the child had to do was leave the rest to the sunshine and, of course, her daily watering. "Two buckets of water a day should do it," said the grandfather as he bent low to his granddaughter. The granddaughter smiled and nodded, admiring their work, and awaiting their bountiful harvest.

Within a few weeks, buds could be seen reaching their tender heads from the brown earth. "Look Grandpa! We have plants!" shouted the little girl with exuberant joy. "How wonderful, my dear, but don't forget, two buckets of water a day to keep them healthy." The child nodded.

Several months later, grandpa came to visit yet again. "How is your garden doing, my dear?" he asked his grandchild. The young girl looked down at the floor, muttering, "It's fine, I guess." Taking the child gently by the hand, grandfather and granddaughter headed to the back yard, only to find a puzzling sight. Half of the garden was green and flourishing and the other half appeared as a desert wasteland! The old man rubbed his chin in bewilderment, then turned to the small child. "Did you water daily, as I instructed, my dear?" he asked. The child replied, "Yes, grandpa, I did." The old man rubbed his chin again. "Did you water it two buckets worth, one for each side?" The child shuffled her feet as she explained the sequence of events. "The first few weeks it was fun to carry the water out and sprinkle the plants, but, after a while, I became tired of carrying those two heavy buckets, so I only used one bucket. There was not enough water for the whole garden, so I only watered half." After a few moments of silence, the grandfather wisely responded," Let us see what we can salvage of this side by watering and fertilizing it. In the meantime, let us harvest the rest."

Real life application: Has something similar to the above scenario happened in your own life? A situation that COULD have been avoided had you properly cared for the events leading to it? For example, think of how many marriages fail due to sheer neglect. Instead of taking the time to care for and "water" these important relationships, it is a sad reality that a large number of divorces occur because some seek a new relationship, rather than tend to the one they committed to before God and man.

The same thing is true in our friendships, work ethics, and various goals in our life. Just as a plant won't grow without sunshine and water, so too will good things NOT come to those who do not work for what they truly desire. God assures us that we are not alone, especially during times of sorrow and hardship. All we have to do is call out to Him and He is faithful to answer the heartfelt prayers of the repentant.

With a little work and a lot of God, nothing is impossible.

Thoughts On Love

Throughout history, man has expressed his thoughts on this thing called "love," sometimes, perceiving it as something wonderful, beautiful, and intense and other times, expressing the sorrow and anger caused by love scorned. Whatever the case, no one can deny that love is a powerful energy and emotion, so intense in fact, that mothers have immediately been overcome with Herculean strength to lift a car or huge boulder off their child.

Let us read what a few past authors had to say on love.

"Love is not what makes the world go round. Love is what makes the trip worthwhile."
-Franklin Jones

"When two people are at one in their innermost hearts, they shatter even the strength of iron or bronze, and when two people understand each other in their innermost hearts, their words are sweet and strong like the fragrance of orchids."
-I Ching

"Love should be a tree whose roots are deep in the earth, but whose branches extend into heaven." - Bertrand Russell

"Man has no choice but to love. For when he does not, he finds his alternative lies in loneliness, destruction, and despair."
-Anonymous

"Loving people are happy, and happy people are loving." - Ken Keyes

"Who would give a law to lovers? Love is unto itself a higher law." - Boethius

"Love is the only gold." -Tennyson

Man may try to understand love and all its effects, but unless he knows the love of God, one can never fully know love, for God IS love, and the gift He gives to us, its foundation, is constructed in love.

It is nice to show our affection to those we love by sending them flowers and candy, or doing kind deeds for them, but true love is not about fleshly desires, or emotions that make our physical bodies feel good, but it feeds the spirit as only God and His son, Jesus Christ can do.

Love has one source and this source is God.

Godly Dentistry

A young business executive was constantly seen in his corporations rest room, peeking in the mirror and fiddling with something in his mouth. As it turns out, the young man suffered from a tooth, which needed immediate repair, yet he repeatedly kept putting it off, instead continually dabbing the sore area with a numbing gel.

Due to neglect, the problem became worse, now infecting a larger portion of the gum area. After one year, the man finally went to the dentist. "I'm sorry," said the dentist," you have a serious infection that has reached to the bone. If we are to salvage that bone, I am going to have to remove several of your teeth and fit you with partial dentures." The young executive was stunned! How could this have happened? How could he have neglected his health like that? he thought. The ointment he had been using killed the pain, but numbing did not solve the deeper problem. And so, the young executive sat back in the dentist's chair to be fitted for his partial dentures.

<u>Real life application</u>: In our own lives, there may be times we prefer to take the easy route and numb the pain through alcohol, drugs, over-eating, or even fleshly pleasures.

Eventually, that quick fix loses its potency and we begin to seek stronger and more powerful pain-killers, yet, all the while the problem is not only being put on hold, but is also worsening due to our neglects.

Stepping away from sin and making a conscious decision to chose godliness is not always easy when we have applied such painkillers to our life, because once the numbing effect wears off, we are then left with a raw nerve. While this now exposed nerve throbs in pain as it cries out for more painkillers, the good news is that we can finally look at the issue face to face, thus begin a road to full recovery.

As our Lord and Savior, our Heavenly Father knows our pains and hears when we cry out to Him and He is quick to respond to those who seek His mercy and gentle guiding hand. He alone is the ultimate Healer.

Letting go of sin is not always easy, but remember, with Jesus Christ, you are never left to deal with healing alone.

Smile!

Syndicated columnist, Ann Landers, recently printed the letter from a woman who wrote to tell about her elderly aunt, who had been greatly blessed, with 108 years on the earth thus far. On one occasion, the wrinkled, yet intellectually robust woman, asked her niece why God keep me all this time?" she asked in puzzlement. Without hesitation, the niece replied," Ida, you're here because of your smile. You have the brightest smile in the world and, when you smile, you make everyone feel good. That's why you're here. You have a purpose." When the elderly woman heard this, she grinned from ear-to-ear, pleased to know her life held some meaning.

I cannot help but apply this quaint story to my own life, for now, when I am out in public, I am much more aware of the facial expressions other people have. Sad to say, there are a lot of people out there with looks of doom and gloom, or sheer indifference.

I don't exactly know what it is about a cheerful look and friendly smile, but this small act can warm one's heart in a unique way. A sincere smile quietly tells the world, "I am happy. I want you to be happy too!" But, a scowl, or a look of indifference, reflects a sentiment of," I am angry and unhappy. I don't care!"

In the Bible, we are told that the countenance of the face reflects what is truly in the heart. *"A happy heart makes the face cheerful, but heartache crushes the spirit." - Proverbs 15:13*

We are also told that real joy and love comes directly from the hand of God. *"To the man who pleases him, God gives wisdom, knowledge and happiness..." -Ecclesiastes 3:26* Thus, it only makes sense, if we want others to see us in a more appealing light outwardly, we must place a profound INWARD light, and the name of that radiant Light is Jesus Christ, the Son of God.

"Your word is a lamp to my feet and a light for my path." - Psalm 119:105

What Are You Eating?

I was reading a book recently, called, "Food and Mood," by author, Elizabeth Somer, M.A., R.D. In this book, the author explores the unique relationship food plays on not only our physical well being, but emotional as well.

Obviously, a healthy and well-balanced diet provides one with optimal health, while a poor diet, one lacking necessary vitamins and minerals, can wreak havoc with our emotional status or mood. One example of this can be in overuse of sugar and caffeine, which is known to make us feel anxious and hyper. With the right diet, certain nutrients in food can improve memory, energy levels, and sleep patterns, weight management, and overall attitude.

There is another great book that also gives us sound information, not on caring for the physical body, but for the spirit. This book is God's Word, the Bible. Take the time to open and read this book and you will see a wonderful guide for optimal spiritual health! Invite Christ into your life and enjoy the satisfying and fulfilling peace, love, and comfort that only He can truly give!

Undying Love

Long-lasting marriages, the "'till death do us part" ones, are not as common as they once were.

Why is this?

Could it be, in our current society, we have grown so used to the fast pace and everything being easily obtained, it has become as easy as tossing a broken toy to the wayside when it breaks, rather than trying to repair it? Has love lost so much value that it can now be boiled down to a few laughs, shared memories, and the temporary thrill of passion? Is this all love is, or is there something more?

The Creator of the universe has already told us exactly what love is. Why on earth would our Maker tell us how to recognize true love? I mean, after all, it IS one of the most basic emotions, isn't it? Do we really NEED God to tell us something we should already know?

Obviously so. Just look at the divorce rate and the statistics on teen pregnancies, spousal abuse, and abortion. Turn on the television and it's almost impossible to avoid some soap opera or talk show where we aren't being exposed to some degree of boastful bed-hopping.

This is what our Creator tells us love is: *"Love is patient, love is kind. It does not envy, it does not boast, it is not proud. It is not rude, it is not self-seeking, it is not easily angered, it keeps no record of wrongs. Love does not delight in evil, but rejoices with the truth. It always protects, always trusts, always hopes, always perseveres. Love never fails."* - I Corinthians 13: 4-8

Notice there is no mention of romance, passion, or physical pleasures. While such things as a candle-lit dinner, long walks on the beach, or a warm embrace may be some of the ways we express and communicate love, they do not represent love in and of themselves. Love that has been injured needs time and great care to mend. When we have a cut or scrape to our knee, do we rub dirt in it? No, we cleanse it and assist it back to health.

So, too, does our Heavenly Father desire us to care for and nurture love so that we can live a more joyous life. God is the great healer and mender of hurting souls. All we need to do is call on Him.

Good Gifts

"The only things we ever keep are what we give away." - Louis Ginsberg

What type of gifts do you like to give your friends and relatives to show them you care, and to let them know how special they are? Would you send a friend a bowl of rotten fruit, or a moth-eaten, tattered, old scarf? No? Then why are we often guilty of giving such thoughtless "gifts" to the person we claim to love the most; our spouse?

Stan and Stella fell in love with each other at first sight. Romance was definitely in the air! Stan was head-over-heels for Stella, and he showed it to her by his kind words and deeds, such as holding the door open for her, and telling Stella how lovely she looked. So too, was Stella wild about Stan, and she would always check her hair and powder her skin so Stan would know how she wanted to look her best for him.

Stan and Stella married; soon to have children. Years passed and the children were leaving home to attend college. On their first day home alone, the alarm rang and Stella silently climbed out of bed in her well-worn flannel nightgown. It was a shabby nightgown, but it was a fond reminder of her deceased mother. With curlers in her hair, and cold cream still on her face from the night before, Stella shook Stan to wake up. With a grunt and grumble, Stan pulled down the covers to begin his day.

As the day progressed, Stella went about her house cleaning. In an old housecoat and rubber gloves, Stella scrubbed and scoured as she listened to the Soap Opera's on television. Stella enjoyed the Soaps because life always seemed so glamorous there. Passion and romance was always in the air, and that seemed all but a memory to Stella. While Stella focused on the house, Stan always seemed to be making some sort of arrangements to go fishing, hunting or some sort of sporting event with his buddies. At home, Stan was quiet and subdued, but with his friends, Stan was often the life of the party, telling jokes, discussing politics and the latest issues of the day. Supper time came and went with few words spoken. A program on the TV watched together, and soon it was lights off and time for bed; Stella in her cold cream and tattered nightie, and Stan who had already turned over and was snoring.

Chances are, Stan and Stella still love each other very much, yet they have slowly

♥ SON Salutations

gotten into the habit of giving each other "poor gifts." The gifts they give to each other are not new, sincere, and well thought out, but are now scraps and remnants. If life were compared to a big pot of stew, Stella and Stan would be feeding each other the burned-on drippings that are crusted on the bottom of the kettle.

What type of gifts have YOU been giving your loved one lately? The finest stew, or the crusty leftovers? If you care for your spouse, then show him by giving him the most precious gift of all, and it will be returned to you many times over!

Just as love can be nurtured in marriage, so too can the love of God bless and refresh our hearts and souls. As our bodies crave to be physically held, so too, do our spirits cry out for the love that only our Heavenly Father can provide. While marital love has it's rewards, the love of God offers the greatest gift: Salvation!

The Ultimate Joy

"Joy is not in things; it is in us." -Benjamin Franklin

What is joy but a gladness of heart! True joy cannot be found in material items or circumstances that may cause a transient smile, such as being on a wonderful vacation or winning the lottery. True joy is internal, not derived from external forces.

How can this be? What great power or force could touch an individual so profoundly that it could replace sadness and discontent with joy and peace?

The answer is God. You see, true joy comes directly from the hand of God because He alone, is Love in its purest form and in genuine love there is joy.

Think for a moment of when you were a child. You lay cradled in your mother's arms, warm, soft, cared for, well loved, and fully nurtured. In her arms, you were safe from all external forces. Close to her breast was your home.

In like manner, our heavenly Father has this special gift to offer those who call on Him in love and sincerity. His Son's victory over death allows us the most profound joy because even though, in our earthy forms, we may face sickness, hardships, even death, nothing can pull us away from His arms or from the salvation He has promised us!

You have not known true joy until you have experienced the heartfelt touch of God!

True Beauty

"Beauty is like the surf that never ceases, Beauty is like the night that never dies, Beauty is like a forest pool where peace is And a recurrent waning planet lies." - Struthers Burt

My grandmother was in her late 80's when she died. Regardless of the effects of age on her body, causing her skin to be withered and wrinkled and her bones not as strong as they once were, I always regarded grandma as a lovely lady.

Grandma had a certain way about her, a manner that was kind, gentle, thoughtful, and very much the character of a true lady. Grandma loved the Lord and loved her family. She was not well educated, but she had a heart of gold and would give the shirt off her back if need be. When I saw grandma lying in her coffin wearing her white pearl necklace and Sunday best dress, I reflected on the life she led and how she had touched so many lives with her simple grace. This was not a physically beautiful woman before me, cancer robbing her of the glow I once knew, yet the contents of grandma's heart, from her very being, seemed to radiate from deep within her.

The beauty grandma held during her life was a

reflection of the love she held, not only within her, but freely gave to all who crossed her path.

As I arose from my kneeling position at her coffin, I could only hope to aspire to the level of beauty this gem of a woman had and, even in her death, so many years after, grandma is still remembered, spoken about, and loved.

<u>Real life application</u>: So many people walk around today worrying about their looks, wondering if they are dressed in the trendiest of clothes, overly concerned if their figure will be appealing to their romantic interest, wanting their teeth to be as white as they can be, etc. How often do we worry about our inner beings or the beauty of our hearts? Is our peaches and cream complexion scowling in hatred and our perfectly lined ruby red lips, spewing vulgarities and malicious lies or gossip?

Our heavenly Father has no regard for outer appearance. What matters to God is the sweetness of our hearts. In time, outer beauty fades, but a heart that has been grounded, rooted, and nurtured in His word and in His love will remain lovely forever! Hold a mirror to your heart. What do YOU see?

Fear: Part 1

H.L. Mencken, author of "Prejudices," has this to say on fear, *"The one permanent emotion of the inferior man is fear - fear of the unknown, the complex, the inexplicable. What he wants beyond everything else is safety."*

Fear is an emotion all men share. We were created with the ability to sense danger and to thereby protect ourselves by allowing this emotion to direct us to safety. For example, it is good and natural to have the feeling of fear when one is standing near a steep cliff. Fear of falling and injuring one's self, or worse, causes us to step back to safety. So too, is fear a mechanism to scare a person away from immoral behavior. For fear of losing one's family, a man tempted to stray from his marriage may reconsider his potentially adulterous actions.

Fear per say is not a bad thing. When it is allowed to become irrational and without basis, then fear becomes an enemy, even an "illness" which plagues many. Whether it's fear of poverty, fear of failure or inadequacy, fear of disease, aging, or death, irrational fears can pull us down emotionally and rob our lives of joy.

♥ SON Salutations

It is not our Creator's desire for His children to live in fear. While a fear of spiders or snakes might not hinder one's life too much, those who experience deeper fears, which reach into every day aspects of their life such as fear of social situations or of growing old, are being slowly robbed of the joy and peace our Creator promises us.

Most of our fears never happen, and of the rest, we can often make these come true ourselves! For example, if we fear failure and walk into a lecture ready to speak with this fear dominating our mind, chances are our own fear will cause us to speak with a lack of confidence.

Many fears are simply the products of our own imaginations and, as we know, the mind can be greatly influenced by our pasts, traumatic circumstances, or some sort of personal issue we have not fully come to grips with. The sooner we realize the basis for irrational fears, the quicker healing is on its way!

People who have such fears tend to not want to reveal these publicly, since they fear it will make them appear insecure, weak, and perhaps "abnormal." Like irrational fears, this feeling of going into hiding with one's weaknesses is just one more form of emotional bondage and entrapment that robs us of the zest for life we COULD have! Fear can turn into a vicious cycle.

Those who fear seek safety and security. Our heavenly Father promises this to those who call on Him. *"So do not fear, for I am with you; do not be dismayed, for I am your God. I will strengthen you and help you; I will uphold you with my righteous hand." (Isaiah 41:10)*

While God wants us to live in peace and comfort, His adversary tries to replace these with darkness, deception, and irrational fear. God wants our joy and freedom and the enemy wants to keep us in bondage.

Do you fear? Then call out to the Father and let Him comfort you as only a loving Father can. Let Him fill you with the love He has for all His children. Reach out, take His hand, and let His truth guide you.

"Never will I leave you; never will I forsake you." (Hebrews 13:5)

Fear: Part II

Eleanor Roosevelt said this about fear, *"You gain strength, courage and confidence by every experience in which you really stop to look fear in the face."*

Facing the roots to one's fear can be a scary thing in itself, for it often entails coming to grips with a painful past or deep insecurities within ourselves. For example, a young child may have had an embarrassing moment during a school play, and during the course of his adult life he develops a fear of public speaking and an apprehension toward any act which places him in center stage. The source of this individuals fear is easily traceable, and sometimes it is something as simple as identifying the foundation of our fears that we can deal with them head on. As it is stated in God's word, *"Then you will know the truth, and the truth will set you free."* (John 8:32)

Once we have insight as to the root of our fears, we then need to make a firm and conscious decision to not let them run our life. Fears that run our lives, also RUIN our life, and it is not God's desire that we live in misery. *"Dear friend, I pray that you may enjoy good health and that all may go well with you, even as your soul is getting along well."* (III John 1:2)

HOW do we replace fear with security? The same way you fill a glass of dirty water with clean, clear water! The more clear and healthy water you pour into the glass, the less dirty water remains. In other words, the more we face the thing we fear, the less frightening it becomes! Just as a baby does not learn to walk overnight, so too, will fear not typically disappear in a moment, but, with the steady and constant feeding of that which is emotionally healthy and godly, the less dark our word becomes. Satan will try to rob us of this light and security, so we must also learn to lean on One who is more able than we are-- Jesus Christ, the Son of God. *"It is better to take refuge in the Lord than to trust in man."* (Psalm 118:8)

There is no shame in admitting our fears and weaknesses, only disgrace in trying to hide our humanity from the ever-watchful eyes of God.

His Comfort

A small child runs down a steep hill, loses his footing, and tumbles the rest of the way down, skinning both his knees on jagged rocks. His father hears the boy's loud sobs, runs to him as quickly as possible, pulls the child to his chest, and comforts him. Once in the house, the father cleanses the wounds and places a band-aid on each knee, as he lovingly, yet sternly, warns his son to be more careful next time. A jagged, rocky hill is not the best place to go running!

Just as the father in this story was there for his son, so too is our Heavenly Father there for us. While our Creator has no greater joy than to see His children prosper and be in good health, He is also there to be a source of peace and comfort in our times of hurt and despair.
We may be adults in an earthly sense, but God knows of our need to still require His gentle and guiding hand and loving care. Truly, He is as a blanket of protection in a hurting world.

Today, open your heart and life to the One who cares about your spiritual welfare, as well as your physical and emotional well-being.

Aging

"Its not how old you are, but how you are old."
-Author Unknown

These last few years have been a time of deep inner reflection for me. You see, I am nearing 40 years old in a few short months and not all of us handle the reality of aging in exactly the same way. While some glide gracefully into middle age, others kick, fight, and scream at every semblance of 'maturity,' pointing angrily at every line, wrinkle, and less-than-firm patch of skin. There came a point though, when I said to myself, "Enough is enough! I am focusing on my self too much! There is nothing I can do to prevent getting older, therefore, I must just *accept* it. There are far worse things to worry about in life than age for goodness sakes! I have my health, family, friends, food, clothing, and shelter. What more could a woman want?" And so, I put the dreaded age monster behind me and continued to simply LIVE.

How easily we can get caught up in trivial matters that seem *huge* at the time. Somewhere in the world, some one has it much worse than our small problem. In some corner of the world, a small child might be starving, an aged person may be on deaths door, or young wife may just be told she has a terminal disease. How silly for us to be so worried about a wrinkle here or there when some people don't know if they will even be seeing another day! If I smile ten thousand smiles and, using those muscles of my face causes me To get another wrinkle, then, I gladly accept it, for I have made Ten thousand people SMILE! If, after another ten or twenty years, my eye lids begin to droop a little, that is OK, for it only means I have looked upon the world in compassion and shed some tender tears. If my hands begin to look dry and frail, it shows that I have been a hard worker and extended my hands to those who needed it.

Age is not a *curse*, but is something very natural, the sign of our growth and potential as human beings. So, too, must we age spiritually, never staying 'spiritual babes,' but forever nourishing our minds and hearts with the truth of His Word so that our spirits can truly flourish and blossom into their fullest potential!

The Cup of Life

(The following inspirational was made in to a play and used to reach children in third-world countries)

A king wanted to test the wisdom of two of the wisest men in his court. Two men were given a silver goblet, each containing equal portions of crystal clear spring water. Each was asked what he saw in the cup. The first man looked and said he saw a half-empty goblet. The second man replied, "My cup is half full." The men were then asked to drink the contents of the cup and relay how drinking the liquid made them feel. The first man complained that the water tasted fine, but there was not enough, he wanted more. The second man then took his turn. "The water tastes good and it has quenched my thirst." The king smiled and, finally, declared who was the wisest man in all his court. "It is you," he said, turning to the second man. Now I will tell you why. Looking to the first man, he said, "The cup represents one's life, the world in which you live. When you looked into the cup, what you saw was a cup half empty, even though the goblet contained the finest spring water in all the land. Instead of sipping and finding satisfaction in its contents, you desired more. In life, you will never see all your many blessings, for your greed and lust for more will always cloud your thinking."

The king then turned to the second man. "When you looked into the cup you saw a cup half full. So, too, will you regard life in this way, reaping all its many blessings and being grateful for the gifts bestowed upon you. A half full cup is not a full cup, yet its contents can still be sweet and satisfying."

The moral of this story is that life is not always perfect, yet how we view our cup will determine what mind frame we have when sipping of its contents.

How many people do you know who feel discontentment in their life? Someone ELSE has the perfect car, job, spouse, or girlfriend, and a generally much more exciting life. Yet, chances are they think YOUR life is better and that it is YOU with the perfect spouse, home, job, etc.

Man, in all his fleshly desires, always wants more. Often this desire for more gets us into trouble, and sometimes we find ourselves losing the very precious things we thought we never had in the first place.

Today, look at your life with new eyes and begin to see the cup half full as opposed to half empty. Do you have food, shelter, clothing? Be thankful, for there are those in impoverished countries who don't even have these basic necessities. Do you have your health, friends, and loved ones who truly care about you? Be grateful, for there are those who lay in hospital beds, suffering and dying with no loved ones to visit and hold their hand.

Lastly, do you have God in your life? Then you are among the richest in the world! If not, it is not too late for Him to fill YOUR cup with His great love and manifold blessings!

Revelations Of Love

"Do not keep the alabaster boxes of your love and tenderness sealed up until your friends are dead. Fill their lives with sweetness. Speak approving, cheering words while their ears can hear them and while their hearts can be thrilled and made happier by them. The kind things you mean to say when they are gone, say them before they go." -Anonymous

Many years ago, as a child, I attended the funeral of a relative. This particular relative was obviously loved, yet those closest to him often spoke ill of him. He was not an openly demonstrative man, but in his own way, he was kind and decent. Behind his back, I heard names to describe him as "bitter, crotchety, and difficult." As the body of this relative lay in the silk-lined casket, his daughter, who was one of those who had a less than desirable relationship with her father, threw herself over his lifeless corpse, sobbed uncontrollably and openly professed how she loved her father. It was a touching and devastating sight for I could not recall a time I ever heard or saw her direct the contents of her heart toward the one who needed to hear it the most. To this day, I do not fully understand why people place flowers and tokens of affection around the body of the deceased. The dead can no longer smell, see, nor hear, so why do we waste our heartfelt emotions? The time to tell our friends and loved ones we care, that they are special and appreciated is when they are alive.

Love is a gift. Unopened, it is nothing. So, too, is the love God has for us, His children, a precious gift. Do not leave it unopened.

A Story About Trust

A poor man prayed in earnest for his family. "Lord, we have depended so much on the kindness of others, now we seek a home to call our own. As you know, my body has become weak from this terrible illness which has finally left me and I have leaned so much on others that I don't even know if I can stand on my own. I ask You, God, for strength of body and spirit, wisdom, and to help provide a home for my darling wife and children." A tear fell down from the man's eye.

A few days later, a kind and elderly widow heard of this father's plight. "I have a plot of land you may have to build upon, but it is sorely overgrown with thick brush, trees, and large rocks. I will gladly give it to you, but it will be a labor-some undertaking," she said. The man also knew this, yet he accepted the widow's generous offer, knowing such an opportunity might not again pass. The man stood afar and surveyed his newly gained property. Looking up, he smiled and said, "Lord, I asked You for a home and You give me this gnarled forest? I will trust and be thankful for the gift before me."

Several days into the major undertaking of leveling the land off, the man slumped against the twentieth tree he cut by hand. Sweat poured from his body, which was now covered by ruddy brown earth. "Lord!" he shouted, "Why did You choose this God-forsaken plot of land? Is this my punishment for not taking care of my family while sick these last few years? Is this the type of loving God You are?" Exasperated, the man clenched his fist and went back to work, muttering to himself, " I will continue to trust."

Several months passed. Upon resting under the final tree to be removed, the man looked about him in wonder. Before him stood a beautiful plot of land to build a home. The lush forest surrounding the leveled area would provide good protection from the cold winter winds and also offer an abundant supply of firewood to keep warm. In a large pile next to the leveled earth, were neatly stacked tree trunks. They would make excellent logs to build a cabin. Ashamed for thinking God had left Him in his most dire time of need, the man rested his head in his hands. Suddenly, he looked in to his palms. These were not the same weak hands that could barely grasp a cup to drink from. Instead, they were strong and fit, as was the rest of his body from the many months of hard physical labor. The man looked up and smiled, saying, "My dear God, thank You. You answered my prayer, even in my worst moments of doubt. You took my weakness and turned it into strength, and my lack of understanding, into wisdom. I will rest a while now, and begin to build my family a house."

The moral of this story concerns faith and trust in God. Often, we ask God for strength and the ability to endure, yet when He offers us more situations to test and try our patience and areas we may need improvement in, we shake our fists, grumble and complain, doubting our Heavenly Father's abilities.

Only God can use our most difficult times to teach us some of our greatest truths. If only we open our hearts and minds, though.

Just as the man in this story trusted God, despite his inability to fully understand from an earthly level, we, too, can see how one may reap the rewards of pure and simple faith and trust in One who is worthy to be called King of Kings and Lord of Lords.

Fresh Starts

While one certainly does not require a particular time to drop unproductive and ungodly habits, now is a wonderful opportunity to set our eyes on a new horizon, here in this dawn of a new millennium.

God is a God of new beginnings and second chances for those who seek a better way. He can transform the most desolate of situations and turn it around to something beautiful. He is the mender of broken hearts, the healer of troubled marriages, and the source of hope in a hurting world.

Thankfully, it is not a complicated task to partake of His blessings and graces. All that is required is genuine desire and faith; faith that not only acknowledges the existence of God, and His Son, Jesus Christ, but faith that He is more than willing and able to touch all aspects of our lives.

When we call on the Lord, do we simply sit back and wait for these expected changes? No! We take action, for believing IS action!

Now is the time to toss away those former unproductive ways, the "poor me" hopeless attitudes, and any sort of ungodliness from our lives. Let them fall away into the past, where they belong, and let us focus our gaze on the

♥ SON Salutations

hope and promise that a new millennium can bring!

Past, Present and Future

In his novel, *A Tale of Two Cities*, Charles Dickens, opens with these famous lines: *"It was the best of times, it was the worst of times, it was the age of foolishness, it was the epoch of belief, it was the epoch of incredulity, it was the season of Light, it was the season of Darkness, it was the spring of hope, it was the winter of despair..."*

While Dickens was referring to life in the 19th century, we can also apply this same sentiment to our entire existence.

Life is in no way stagnant, but, as thinking human beings, the emotions and experiences we encounter in an entire lifetime can most definitely run the gamut. The fact is, in our life, we will encounter pain as easily as pleasure and sadness as quickly as happiness. Along with wise decisions, there will be mistakes and poor choices. The same mouth that can utter soothing words of love and comfort can occasionally spew hatred and bitterness. We can rejoice in our gladness and fret in our despair, yet, through it all, the good times and the bad times, it is part of who we are and the fact we are not cold, unemotional, robots, but feeling humans who have been given the gift of intelligence and free will.

♥ SON Salutations

Our Creator gave us these gifts because He had no desire to make us as obedient puppets on a string and, when something goes wrong, we often fail to take responsibility for the choices we ourselves made. We shake our fists and cry out, "Why me, God?"

As we sow, so shall we reap.

I have made plenty of mistakes; yet, there comes a time when we must learn to let go of the hurts and disappointments, the opportunities lost, and all things negative that keep us looking back rather than gazing forward. If we call on God in earnest prayer, and claim to have repented of the past, then why do we refuse to let go? If God is faithful to His word, then the mistakes of our past are long forgotten as a slate is wiped clean of its chalk marks.

Just as Charles Dickens seemed to make peace with the dual nature of the 19th century in all its advances and turmoil, so, too, does our Heavenly Father see the good and evil within our lives and He is quick to forgive those who call upon Him in repentance so that we may truly make peace with the past and get on with the future.

Perspectives

Today began like any other day. In the course of several hours, though, I found my self sitting in a hospital emergency room awaiting the diagnosis of my husband, who had been suddenly stricken by a problematic gall bladder.

As my spouse waited to be admitted into the hospital for surgery, I could hear other emergency room patients relaying to doctors and nurses of how sickness had also befallen them. One brawny man, whose arms were covered with tattoos, was reduced to a helpless child, his asthma so severe he could barely speak. Another man, who had advanced Multiple Sclerosis, came in to seek relief from agonizing headaches he would get sporadically. Across from us, lay a grossly overweight woman who had a stroke. Even though my husband and I were there with this matter of his gall bladder, after hearing so many stories of tragedies, I was thankful it was nothing more serious.

That night, as my husband was recuperating from surgery, I walked about the hospital looking for a coffee machine. I stumbled upon the ward where terminal patients were housed. These people were at death's door with terminal diseases, such as AIDS and

Leukemia. Compared to these patients, my husband's emergency gall bladder removal was insignificant. Instead of asking, "Why God?" I began saying, "Thank you, God!"

How easy it is to lose our perspective on matters of ill health and tragedy. Somewhere in the world someone else has it MUCH worse.

When tragedy strikes, there is nothing we can do to turn back the hands of time. We must accept the situation and deal with it practically, head on. At the same time, we must call out to God for his strength, guidance, and hand of protection. As with all things, God's will be done. We might not understand it in our lifetime, but we can still place our faith and trust in His heavenly wisdom so that even in the darkest of tragedies, His light will always shine through.

More Beauty Lessons

Think of your first love. Didn't the world seem brighter and much more joyous when love was in full swing within your heart? Didn't those around you see an almost continual smile on your face and eyes brimming with love and happiness?

How do your friends, associates, and loved ones see you today? Has life been slowly drained from your eyes?

In the Bible, we are told that the eyes are the window to your soul. In other words, the essence of one's being is reflected in the outer appearance.

Think how you walk when you are in a good mood and things are going your way. Your stance is tall, straight, and you walk with a bounce in your step. But what about when life has thrown you a few punches and you're feeling depressed? Chances are, you're walking sluggishly with posture slumped as if the weight of the world were on your shoulders.

While the reality of an earthly existence can never compare to that of our heavenly reward, it is not God's desire for man to live in despair.

♥ SON Salutations

Love and joy IS very much attainable by working toward such things, never losing grasp of our goals, dreams, and hopes, AND through our walk with God and His Son Jesus Christ.

Even though the path may sometimes be bumpy, HE is always there to be our strength, comfort, and salvation!

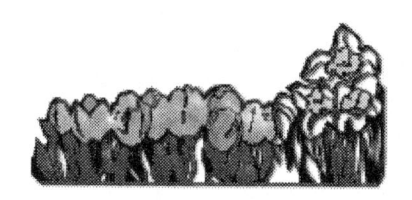

Planning

My husband and I are still in the prime of our lives, yet we are beginning to seriously discuss our impending retirement. As a newly married couple, when my spouse tried to raise the issue of old age, financial security, and death, I was not as open to discussing such topics at length. They were often painful and I felt there was more than enough time to ponder such things. But as I now approach my 40's and my husband his 50's, I know that, as painful as it is, we must face age for there is no way to avoid it. Thus, it is best to prepare, plan, and make the most of it by doing things now that will ensure our optimal health and well-being for later.

So many times we plan and prepare for our earthly future, yet give little regard to our spiritual welfare and future. And, just as there are some individuals who reserve thoughts of old age for when they are seniors, suddenly finding them self unprepared, so too, do some people put off thoughts of God and salvation until they are facing serious trauma, illness, or death.

Why put off for tomorrow what you can do today? Call on Christ and ensure your future.

Balance

If we think of our body as a large scale, we can see how body, mind, and spirit can balance, each facet of our very being in complete symmetry.

How easy it is for this scale to become unbalanced though. For example, if we overindulge our body with food and drink we can see how our scale tips off kilter bringing about a state of physical ill health. And what about our minds? Obsessing, stressing, and filling our minds with ungodly thoughts can also make our scale lean too heavily to one side.

So too, is the need to balance our spiritual facets. Neglected or not properly fed, our scale tips and this hunger is left empty, thus forming a void. The void then becomes easy target for false truths, spiritually unhealthy practices and the like.

God wants us to prosper and be of good health. It is not His desire for us to be malnourished and unbalanced. Perhaps, today is a good day to check YOUR scales of balance, removing that which is UN-godly, and feeding that which cries out for God.

Ambition

Our world is often very success oriented. We are told we must be ambitious and fight for wealth, status, and recognition.

Desiring a pleasant life and the development of one's skills to their maximum potential is all well and fine, but how much importance do we place on our spiritual ambitions? Does a new house take precedence than one's salvation? Are you more willing to buy a book or take a course in personal improvement or financial success than gaining an understanding of your Creator?

It is true that some individuals have no spiritual ambition at all, seeking only to satisfy their flesh and ignoring the needs of the spirit and threatening their very salvation.

In the Bible we are told there is a way that seems right to man, but in the end, they are the ways of death. Flesh seeks to please the needs of the flesh, while the spirit hungers for soul food. Desiring to care for our earthly bodies is indeed noble, but don't deprive your soul of its salvation in the process. By putting God First, all other things fall nicely into place.

Never Alone

I recall reading with great shock and wonder of some individuals, mostly teens, who were so disturbed with their life they felt a need to mutilate their bodies by pulling out their hair, bruising their skin, or slashing their flesh with a razor. Those individuals willing to speak openly about this revealed they felt so numb and empty inside that the pain of the self-injury simply confirmed they were indeed alive and could still feel. I could not help but wonder if the emptiness they spoke of was the result of lack of God in their lives. Did the absence of spiritual nurturing leave each feeling like life held no real purpose other than to eat, drink, be merry, and then fall to one's eventual death? Under this mind set, it's no wonder one is left with a sense of purposelessness, even hopelessness.

It is not our Heavenly Father's desire for us to be ignorant about our spiritual welfare, nor for us to be estranged from His divine presence. If we feel a void from Him, it is not because He has turned His back on US, but WE who have ignored and rejected HIM and His Word. Problems in life will always be there, but with God on our side we will never be..alone.

Ocean

While on vacation in Florida, I walked along the ocean shore collecting shells and enjoying the early morning coolness. As the clear surf rhythmically crashed over the rocks and sand, I looked into the distance to the seemingly never-ending blanket of water. I knew there was an end to the ocean, the other side of it, but from where I stood, no end was in sight.

Isn't this exactly how troubles in our life often appear as we tend to focus on the expanse of our inevitable problems, ignoring the end in sight? Like the ocean, in all earthly things, there is a beginning and an end. So, too, with every sadness, conflict, or hardship, there will follow a resolution and an end. With every storm comes the sun afterwards.

In the Bible, God tells us that, although we may feel alone, we are not. Our Heavenly Father is there to hold our hand, to comfort and offer peace to a hurting world.

If you are going through a difficult period in your life, now is the time to call on Christ. The end to your problem will not be so far off and it will be the beginning of a new relationship with Christ!

Beauty Lessons

A summer excursion to the beach brought me to notice all the "sun worshippers" who lay basking in the sweltering heat in an attempt to beautify their appearance with a bronze-color hue. As I joined the sun-bunny crowd for the day-- my excuse being that I had to watch my children as they splashed about in the water-- I began to think of all I had read about the damaging affects of the sun on human skin, such as premature aging, denser and tougher skin texture, and a higher risk of skin cancer. Are we that vain we are willing to risk our health for beauty's sake?

God does not care about the outer appearance, for it is only a temporary casing and not a true reflection of the entire being. While the outer only reveals beauty, the inner holds one's true heart and character.

Today is a good day to think about who we are trying to please: God or man?

Only ONE offers salvation.

Forgiveness

Eight year old Henry was labeled "precocious" by most who knew him. Where trouble lurked, Henry was never far off. One particular Saturday, Henry's family decided to devote the afternoon to Spring cleaning. Henry wasn't too thrilled about scrubbing, dusting, and polishing, but the thought of being able to rummage through boxes of odds n' ends excited him. Who knows what treasures could lurk in an unsuspecting crate?!

Henry's first stop was the dining room to help mom unpack some fine china figurines, of great-grandma's, his mom inherited. Henry was careful in unwrapping the interesting looking figurines, but, when he caught a glimpse of a clown head, he became so excited his arm swung out and sent the expensive nic-nac crashing against the wall. "Henry!" mother yelled, "Look what you did! Go help your father instead!" Henry felt very bad, but took a deep breath and headed off to the garage.
It wasn't long before Henry once again had his hand in trouble. The sight of Henry holding the hammer and dad holding his throbbing red thumb, while sputtering incoherent sounds, said it all. Henry sighed and headed back into the house. On the way up the stairs to his bedroom, he accidentally stepped on the cat's

♥ SON Salutations

tail sending poor kitty running and screeching.

Night came and supper sat ready on the table. The whole house sparkled. Every one was at their place, everyone but Henry. Mother called out Henry's name, but no one answered. Henry's dad went up stairs, but Henry's room was empty. Henry's family began searching high and low, but just when hope was getting low, there was Henry, hiding in his closet. It was obvious he had been crying. "Henry!" cried mom, "Why are you hiding?" Henry responded quietly, "Because I can't do anything right. Everyone yells at me even when I say sorry for an accident." Mother crouched down and hugged Henry. "Oh my poor darling!" she said, squeezing him harder, "WE are the ones who are sorry right now! We let our tempers get the best of us, and said thoughtless things which hurt your feelings. It was wrong of us and we are sorry." Dad and the rest of the family nodded their heads in agreement. Henry looked up, wide-eyed, and in a cheerful tone said, "You mean YOU all made a mistake and are asking MY forgiveness?" Mother smiled and nodded her head. "Cool!" shouted Henry as he got up and darted downstairs to eat, just missing kitty's tail.

The lesson of this story is that no human is

perfect; we all have weaknesses, shortcomings, and make mistakes. Jesus did not come for the perfect, but for the hurting, those who have stumbled and fell. Through God and His Son, Jesus Christ, we can have forgiveness, as our heavenly Father is merciful. Let not only His love dwell in you, but forever keep the knowledge that if He forgives 'us,' we too, must forgive others.

"But because of his great love for us, God, who is rich in mercy, made us alive with Christ even when we were dead in transgressions - it is by grace you have been saved." - Ephesians 2:4-5

Diets

The human body is an intricate creation, feeding itself from nutrients found in our food sources. Science has proven that a diet lacking in a necessary vitamin or mineral can send the body into a state of inefficiency and general ill health.

Just as our physical bodies sometimes aren't running as well as they could, so too does our emotional well being occasionally suffer when we aren't fed a diet of good things. For example, pouring hatred, bitterness, and constant stressful circumstances into one's life, on a steady basis, is known to most definitely affect an individual, making one more susceptible to such physical and emotional ailments as ulcers, high blood pressure, nervous breakdowns, etc.

What type of diet are YOU feeding those you love? Do you give generously of yourself, offering love, care, and warmth on a silver platter? Or do you dish out a diet of fast food scraps?

In the Bible, God speaks of returning to our first love. While this particular verse was relating to our relationship with Jesus Christ so, too, can we learn another valuable lesson in regards to neglecting our loved ones and THEIR need of our love and attention.

Just as our family life will begin to deteriorate when we don't nurture and nourish it, equally will our relationship with Christ when we turn our back on our Heavenly Father.

Be of good health and call on Christ today!

Continued Education

Summer fun in the sun is over and now it is time for children to get serious and hit the books. Of course, children will not be the only ones to advance in their education. High school and college age students are also back into a learning mode, as are adults who are enrolled in continuing education courses.

The ability to learn, grow, and better ourselves is a wondrous gift we have been given! How fortunate in that we do not have to stagnate in our learning and physical abilities just because we reach a certain age. I know of individuals who have switched careers in midlife and broke loose of the tired molds society can often negatively put on an individual.

Life has so much to offer if we only have the desire to reach for it! So, too, does one's spiritual growth need to be watered and nurtured so that we do not remain mere babes in our knowledge and understanding, but mature adults. The knowledge is readily available in God's word, the Bible.

Learn something new today. Call on God.

Art Lessons

"The canvas of your life is painted by the colors we choose from the pallet of everyday living... and sometimes it's not a pretty picture." -Alan Campbell

If you had to paint a picture which reflected your life at this very moment, what would your canvas look like? Would it have light, airy-looking pastel flowers reminiscent of happiness and pleasantness? Warm red hearts portraying love? Angry or sad looking slashes of black scattered with no purpose?

How the "picture" of our life appears is reflected by what we choose to put on our canvas. While we may THINK we have little control over what colors we will paint with, the reality is that God says otherwise. You see, this is why our Heavenly Father issued man the Bible, to be used as a guidebook; a way to know what is a blessing in His sight, and what is an abomination, what will bring one joy and salvation, and what will render one miserable and lead one to eternal damnation.

God is a caring Father, desiring our canvas to be lovely and pure. When we venture outside of the lines He has set forth, guidelines that any truly caring parent would set forth for His

♥ SON Salutations

children, we should not wonder why our "picture" looks flawed and unpleasant.

Today, call out to God for a gift; a gift that can only be achieved through His Son, Jesus Christ. The gift is salvation, a new lease on life, a new canvas. This time, choose your colors wisely.

Whistling

As a child living in my parents home in a rural suburb of upstate New York, I can recall my father who was a rugged and devoted husband and father. While mom cooked, cleaned, and took care of the inside of the house, dad spent all of his free time tending to the outside chores as cultivating our large garden, mowing the lawn, and general tinkering with some sort of mechanical repair of one sort of another in the basement. I noticed, even back then, that dad always seemed to be whistling. It was a comforting and pleasant sound and one that drew me to occasionally join him or, at the minimum, tap my toe or quietly hum to my self as I went about my own chores.

Did you know it takes effort to whistle? It's not that putting your lips together and blowing is so hard, but it seems to me that the important ingredient to whistling is JOY.

Think about the times you have whistled in your life. You were happy and in a good mood, right? The joy within you was as a fountain begging for release. You wanted it to flow, so out from your lips came the joy within you, the sweet sound of music, whistling.

In the Bible, we are told that through our faith

in God we may obtain joy. *("You have made known to me the path of life; you will fill me with joy in your presence, with eternal pleasures at your right hand." - Psalm 16:11)*

The joy of His servants may be full! *("My servants will sing out of the joy of the joy of their hearts, but you will cry out from anguish of heart and wail in brokenness of spirit." -Isaiah 65:14)*

You see, what is in our hearts comes through our mouths and actions. When one is filled with bitterness and hatred, his mouth will spew hate and his deeds will not be loving, but when one has real joy in his heart, the spirit rejoices and wants to share the happiness that is within.

Real joy can only come from God. Certainly, the carnal world can offer cheap imitations from money and fame, but TRUE joy only comes from knowledge of God and the salvation only He can offer through His Son, Jesus Christ.

Garbage Men

Stan was a garbage man, otherwise known by the politically correct term of "sanitation worker." Strangely, Stan loved his job! Garbage was in his blood. Every morning, at the crack of dawn, Stan would take his place on the small step at the back of the truck. Down the street, Stan's truck would roll, stopping at every house, Stan, jumping down, grabbing the large tin receptacles, emptying them and hopping back on to the truck. On his sleeves, egg shells, coffee grounds, week old spaghetti would drip. Treasuring the smells and stains, Stan would wear the same dingy, old overalls week after week even wearing them at home or while out and about on daily errands. Stan could not understand why everyone seemed to slowly back off when he stood near.

One day, Stan decided he had enough of living in garbage. Still un-bathed, still wearing his smelly, stained overalls, fingernails as black as ever, Stan went to the finest executive offices in the best side of town. Through the pristine marble building Stan walked, all ready to set his life in trash aside and start anew. "I am here for a job," Stan told the stunned secretary as she held her nose and cringed her eyes while gazing at the reeking figure before her.

♥ SON Salutations

"You have got to be kidding!" shouted the secretary as she discretely hit the button for security to haul Stan away. "Look at you!" she yelled, "You are filthy, disgusting, and smell like raw sewage! Why in the world would we want to hire YOU?!" she continued. A tear slid down Stan's cheek and, without a word, he walked out of the room back to his future in trash which he knew so well.

The above story is, of course, fictional. The purpose of this illustration is to show this is exactly how WE appear to God when we approach Him for forgiveness; our souls are blackened with sin, flesh reeking with the scent of evil. Out of our mouths spew lies, hatred, and vulgarities. We come to God in this horrible condition, with arms outstretched and, in essence, say, "Hold me! Love me! Care for me!" Does our heavenly Father, in all His purity and goodness, back off? No...He welcomes us with open arms and says, "Yes, I will love you. I will keep you."

What a great and loving Father God is! So loving, in fact, that He has no greater joy than to extend His arms to His children.

Let God cleanse your soul today.

No Place Like Home

"Somewhere Over The Rainbow" is the theme song of the famous musical production, "The Wizard Of Oz." In this song, Dorothy sings of a place of pleasantries, a sort of Utopia, where no sadness, only gladness exists. By the end, after going through many upsetting ordeals, Dorothy's only desire is to get back to the safety and comfort of her own very real backyard. She whispers over and over, "There's no place like home. There's no place like home," as she is awakened to find her ordeal may have all been just a bad dream.

How many people do you know who are living their life like Dorothy, searching for something that exists only in their own imagination when all along their real happiness has been right before them in their own backyard? For example, there are those people who hold unrealistic expectations in their personal relationships or marriage, seeking the perfect Adonis, the type or person who only exists in romance novels and fantasies. This perfect individual never has a bad hair day or bad breath and never loses his temper or forgets a special occasion.

Today, divorce rates are astronomical. The pedestal we once placed our marriage vows on has sunk to footstool proportions, partially due to the fact our society is used to tossing something aside when it is broken rather than take time to repair the problem.

Marriage is a commitment and should never be entered into lightly; it is real work and takes the devotion of both partners if it is to succeed.

In the Bible, God tells us ALL things are possible to those who place their faith in God and His Son Jesus Christ. If God created the earth and all living things in six days, was able to perform wondrous miracles and raise His Son from the dead, would it be too difficult for Him to repair a hurting marriage?

It is not God's intention for a long, committed, and happy marriage to be something that exists only in one's dreams. There truly CAN be "no place like home" if husband and wife place their faith and trust, not only in each other, but in the capable and loving hands of our Heavenly Father, God.

Call on Him today.

Old Joe

Old Joe was the local derelict. No one really knew the cause of what sent him to the streets It was rumored he only had an elementary education. His disheveled and dirty appearance made him seem older than his 30 years. When he would walk by, people would whisper behind his back saying, "Poor old Joe. Will nothing good come of him?"

Old Joe spent his days searching in garbage cans for redeemable bottles and his nights sleeping in an alley.

One day, Joe seemed to disappear without a trace. Some thought he hopped a train to the south, but no one knew for sure.

Ten years later, a new preacher came to town; he had a quiet and relaxed way about him as he stood on the corner handing leaflets out. On occasion, he could also be seen treating a homeless person to lunch as they sat and talked and he was also a favorite guest speaker at the local church. After one sermon, a group of elderly ladies gathered together, commenting on how wise the preacher was. "Obviously, he came from a very good college," remarked one lady. "Yes, it is rumored he came from a very well to do family," said another.

♥ SON Salutations

The following Sunday, the preacher began to speak, "Ten years ago I felt I was a nobody. I had no real family, a limited education, and couldn't get a job. No one seemed to care, so I, too, began to not care about my self. A woman reached out to me one day, told me about someone who DID care, God. She told me that God does not look at the outer appearance, but at one's heart. She told me that He loved me so much He sent His Son to die on the cross for my sins and that, through Him, I could have salvation." The preacher continued, "On that day, my life changed dramatically because for once I had a sense of hope. I may not have had an earthly family, but I had a whole slew of 'brother's and sister's' in the family of Christ! No longer did I have to be 'poor old Joe,' be cause in the Bible, it told me I was now a child of God! (*"How great is the love the Father has lavished on us, that we should be called children of God!" I John 3:1)*" The whole congregation sat and stared in awe, now knowing the distinguished man before them was 'ole Joe. That day, the sharing of his story of faith, hope, and love changed many lives.

Through the example of Old Joe, we can know that through God, former things are passed away and the new is now upon us!

High On Christ

A 1993 survey reported that illicit drug use among 8th graders is on the rise. At such a ripe and promising time in their lives, what causes not only a teen, but any individual for that matter, to desire to escape from reality and descend to the subculture of drug dependency-- a life which enslaves one to the very substance that claims to offer temporary pleasure?

True happiness and meaning to life cannot be found in a bottle or a pill. Those who use drugs, alcohol, food, or even the abuse of one's sexuality, in an attempt to find joy or purpose, are utilizing cheap imitations and failing to recognize "the real thing." You see, in a large sense, much of our society has removed the purpose for living which is God-centered. Without God, what remains is a bleak existence of feeding our fleshly desires; yet in our deepest inner being, our soul continues to cry out to be nourished with spiritual food, God.

Isn't it about time we set the substances down and sought a different type of "high," the true glory that comes with facing heavenward?

Letting Go

Barbara Streisand sang a song titled, "The Way We Were." In it, she speaks of past love, past experiences, and letting go of the painful past. The song concludes with a positive message, that being to focus on the good and what was learned as a result, yet to let go of the hurts, pains, and disappointments so one may be free to grow.

So often, we let the hurts of the past bring us down and keep us in bondage. We blame our shortcomings on a bad childhood, or an addiction on our genes. We point fingers at distant shadows from the past, yet often fail to point a critical finger at the responsibility we have for our own lives.

What has already happened is called "the past" for a good reason. It is an event or events which have already taken place and are over and done with.

Living in the past and not letting go is not a natural or healthy state of mind. Replaying hurtful memories, whether they occurred twenty years ago, last month, or last week, will slowly destroy one's spirit and that is not what God has in mind for you.

Today is a good day to release the chains of bondage that might be holding you back. Let go of all evil.

The past is past, today is here and now, and the future will come soon enough.

True Wisdom

So many people today claim to have knowledge and the key to all understanding. For them, to admit otherwise is to admit weakness.

In the Bible, we are told that true wisdom only comes from God. In many ways, one can regard the constant struggle for truth as a war of sorts as humans seem to continually be battling between the dictate of man, as opposed to the divine word of God. Those who reject God will also shun His word so true wisdom becomes temporarily unavailable. I say "temporarily" because, thankfully, God is faithful to His word and those who call on Him will always be answered. *"The fear of the Lord is the beginning of knowledge, but fools despise wisdom and discipline."* (Proverbs 1:7)

While humankind often places material items, wealth, and success in very high regard, God tells us in His word that wisdom is even better than silver or gold! *"How much better to get wisdom than gold, to choose understanding rather than silver!"* (Proverbs 16:16)

Being the loving father He is, God made it easy for us to attain spiritual wisdom. He gave us His word then presented mankind with a living testament of His word, Jesus Christ, the

♥ SON Salutations

Son of God. The more we read, the more we understand. The better we understand, the better we can love and increase our faith!

How long will we shun knowledge? How long will we reject God? Take a step toward wisdom today and accept Christ as your Lord and Savior.

Truth Prevails

Several years ago, a college student said to me, "That's all well and fine you have your faith, but why can't you just keep quiet about it?" I explained to the young man that I was not being obnoxious or overbearing in my spiritual beliefs, but since we had been discussing topics which warranted truthful answers, it would have been unkind of me to hide the truth from him. Again he chimed, "Yes, but that's YOUR truth. My truth may be different from yours." "Wrong," I replied, "Truth is truth and knows no boundaries."

Without a strong foundational basis of truth, we are left to our own devices, groping in the dark for some semblance of righteousness. These ideas or practices, such as many of crystal healings, predicting the future with tarot cards, past life regression "therapy," and the like, pull one farther away from truth rather than bring one closer.

In the Bible, Jesus says, *"I am the way and the truth and the life. No one comes to the Father except through me." (John 14:6)* Simply put, we worship Christ because He is worthy to be worshipped. We believe in God's word because He is worthy to be believed. We praise the Lord because He is worthy to be thanked and praised. My soul rejoices because He has provided those who believe in Him with comfort, peace, and joy. Together, we exalt His name because He tells us repeatedly, in the Bible, to go teach the masses of His glory. This is not an act of pride or boastfulness, but a gesture of true care and love.

My conversation with the college student ended on a positive note, that being we both came to the agreement Christ's purpose was not financially lucrative or success-oriented, nor were his kind gestures selfish, uncaring, or unmerciful. Indeed, the young man and I concluded that if one had to select one word to describe Christ, that word would be love, a term no New Age practice could genuinely live up to. Not only was Christ's motive love, it is only through Him that we may have salvation and eternal life. "You know," said the college student, "This Jesus dude just might be worth looking into more." I smiled and nodded my head.

Miss Norma

This is a true story based on my interview with Norma McCorvey.

A middle-aged woman named Norma expressed that she felt like the walls of the church would crumble when she took the first steps to know Jesus Christ in the summer of 1995. At one time, Norma was steeped in a life of drinking, drugs, sexual immorality and confusion. Today, 'Miss Norma' (as she likes to be called) is sober and has a totally different outlook on life. "God has just gotten into my heart," she states. What's more, she is now a staunch supporter of the pro-life movement. What makes this last statement significant is that most people may better know Miss Norma as "Jane Roe," the former plaintiff in the 1973 Supreme Court ruling of "Roe V Wade" on abortion. What is most inspiring about this 49 year old woman's story is that her conversion to Christianity is viable proof of how Christ can so completely turn around a life when there is true repentance and a desire to do what is acceptable in the sight of God.

The Bible relays that *"whosoever shall call upon the name of the Lord shall be saved." (Romans 10:13)* We are also told that the Lord is rich in mercy to those who call upon Him (Ephesians 2:4-5). Like billions of others who have barely escaped eternal damnation in Hell, Miss Norma's initial apprehension when entering church was due to the realization that she, like all of us, are sinners, and that it is only through God's grace that we may be saved.

It is not an easy task to admit that we have failed God. Thankfully, God is not there to condemn those who cry out to Him, but to rejoice and tenderly guide us into His loving arms.

When there is genuine remorse for transgressions of the past, there is a desire for a better way. A way that is pure and acceptable in God's eyes. And like Miss Norma's dramatic turn-around, the Bible declares that *"if any man be in Christ, he is a new creature: old things are passed away; behold, all things are become new." (II Corinthians 5:17)*

What a truly great and loving Father we have!

Legacies

"I would rather be ashes than dust! I would rather that my spark should burn out in a brilliant blaze than it should be stifled by dry rot. I would rather be a superb meteor, every atom of me in a magnificent glow, than a sleepy and permanent planet. The function of man is to LIVE, not to exist. I shall not waste my days trying to prolong them. I shall use my time."
-Jack London

What is your legacy? In other words, how will others remember you once you have walked your last step and taken your final breath? Will your children recall a loving and involved parent or one who always seemed too immersed in work to be bothered? What about your spouse? Will your time together be remembered warmly or will bitter thoughts of constant conflict take precedence? How about friends, relations, and associates? Will they hold fond memories of an individual with great character or will some other not-so-desirable trait be recalled?

How many of us are doing, exactly, what the last line of Jack London's credo states and merely "existing" rather than "LIVING?"

Our heavenly Father did not give us five

senses so we may let them stagnate. While we are not to let our flesh and senses dominate our life, there is no harm in using and enjoying what our Creator graciously gave us to use for our enjoyment and pleasure, within the bounds of His Word. Indeed, by using our senses and ability to love, we may be better stewards of His word! You see, it is in seeing the beauty in the small, unassuming things that one can fully appreciate the bigger picture!

Open your eyes and see all He created! Breathe in the aroma of all His diverse flora! Appreciate the sound of a young child's innocent laughter and take refuge in the warm embrace of someone who cares! Lastly, look heaven-ward, not only at the clouds and stars, but towards the radiant light of our Father, God.

Men Of Sorrow

"Believe me, every man has his secret sorrow which the world knows not and, often times, we call a man cold when he is only sad."
-Henry Wadsworth Longfellow

Happiness. Sadness. Both emotions are an inevitable part of life. We rejoice over our successes and share these happy moments freely with others, but what do we do with our miseries, disappointments, regrets, fears, and worries? Happiness is an easy thing to share, but sadness, most often, is a cold and lonely road, for, it is during these times, one must expose weakness and vulnerability. (*"My guilt has overwhelmed me like a burden too heavy to bear."* - Psalm 38:4)

Why are we so afraid to admit we are human, that we cannot possibly carry all the burdens of the world and that there WILL be times our knees will weaken from too heavy a load?

It is not God's intention for us to carry our burdens alone. In the Bible, we are told to cast our troubles to the Lord. (*"Cast your cares on the Lord and he will sustain you..."* - Psalms 55:22) Although we may be weak due to our fleshly nature, He alone is strong and can offer comfort. We are also not to let those who are burdened with sorrow handle their troubles alone, but we are, instead, instructed to bear one another's burdens and be true keepers of the 'golden rule.'

("Love your neighbor as yourself." -Galatians 5:14)

Jesus Christ, the Son of God, knew sorrow and suffering all too well. Read what the Bible says about this: *"He was despised and rejected by men, a man of sorrows, and familiar with suffering. Like one from whom men hide their faces, he was despised and we esteemed him not. Surely, he took up our infirmities and carried our sorrows, yet we considered him stricken by God, smitten by him, and afflicted. But he was pierced for our transgressions, he was crushed for our iniquities; the punishment that brought us peace was upon him, and by his wounds we are healed."* - Isaiah 53:3-5)

Do not dwell in your sorrows alone, but turn them over to One who truly knows, understands, and can ease your pains, not to mention most importantly, can offer you salvation!

United In Light

"It is better to light a candle than to curse the darkness. And many of us have lit our small candles. But always we were aware of the shadowed corners. When we discovered we could light our candles together, the darkness vanished. Our Father's work is done when we together, with joy, bring our gifts, however small, to be used by those God chooses to bear His light."
-Light of the World by Aimee' Jeanne Garlich

The above poem reveals a great truth that people need each other. One candle in the darkness is effective, though still a small thing, many candles brought together can light a much larger area.

In this world we live in, how easy it is to feel like a cold stone tower standing erect in a vast wilderness. Regarding ourselves as a fortress of strength, we often isolate from the outside world, and, sadly, in the process, turn our back on the One who created us, God. We turn our emotions inward instead of outward. Nothing passes these cold, hard walls for, in essence, we have unknowingly become our own 'god.' We need no one and no one needs us. Or so we think.

In the Bible, we are told that God is love. God loved so much that He created mankind. He loved so much, He also sacrificed His Son for our sins. You see, God gave man a great gift and this is our ability to love. God reached out to man and we, too, must reach out to each other. The more one gives of his love, of himself, the more we begin to understand what true love is about; it is not fleeting pleasures, but truth, peace, and caring.

Within each of us are special small gifts. It is not our heavenly Father's intention for us to selfishly horde these talents, but to use them and share them for the betterment of mankind, so that all people may experience love. The smallest gestures often have the most profound affects. Just look at how the death of one man (Jesus Christ) shed light on an entire world filled with darkness.

Do not hide your love. Reach out to God and others.

Commitment

The dictionary defines commitment as an agreement or pledge. In days gone by, it was not uncommon for a deal or agreement to be solidified solely by a handshake. When a man said his word was as good as gold, he meant it. To break his word showed lack of character and no man desired to have his integrity questioned.

Today, it seems an individual's word no longer holds the great importance it once did. Pledges, agreements, deals, and vows are broken routinely, be it in the business or financial realm, or in the sanctity of the marital union.

What of our spiritual commitments? Do we tell God we believe in Him and love Him, yet continually break the very laws we proclaim to hold dear? Or worse yet, have we failed to even MAKE a commitment to our Heavenly Father?

Committing one's life to Christ is not a burden; it is as simple as confessing in our hearts that Jesus Christ is Lord and Savior of our life. It also means we are not ashamed or embarrassed of our faith, but we proudly stand righteousness sake.

A true commitment does not need a pen or legal document, but a sincere desire to make good on one's word.

Today, commit your life to Christ!

Tomorrow

There is a song by the popular music group Fleetwood Mac entitled, "Don't Stop Thinking About Tomorrow." This sentiment is quite contrary to how our current generation often lives, since most of us tend to exist solely for today, the here and now. Without concern for what tomorrow may hold, many live their lives as if they are walking along a narrow trail in a dense forest. On such a path, one cannot see what dangers lurk or stand before them. All that can be seen is the beauty and pleasure within the immediate visual realm. If one is not careful, a seemingly unassuming path can lead right off a deadly cliff.

In the Bible, we are told not to give too much worry for tomorrow, but, in the same breath, it is certainly not our Heavenly Father's intention for us to be ignorant about one's future either. For decisions we make today can determine where we will spend our eternity.

Do you desire to spend your eternity with God, to partake of the salvation only His Son Jesus Christ can offer? If so, then don't just live for today, lift your head up, see the big picture, and, as the song goes, "don't stop thinking about tomorrow."

Unexpected Results

Our family and 19 others were initiated into the new year by a devastating fire that left many in our apartment building without homes. Our family was blessed to not have lost anything, just inconvenienced by having to relocate. The management staff of our complex was very accommodating and offered all those affected by the fire temporary housing at a local hotel, as well as 3 meals a day. Each day, most of the families would gather in the hotel lobby, discussing their losses as well as plans for the future. What amazed me was that most of the individuals, some losing everything they had ever worked for and left with only the clothes on their backs, retained a very positive attitude. Here were professional business men and women, homemakers, and college students who barely had time to utter a single hello, and here we all were, talking, laughing, sharing meals and fellowship together. I was impressed at how these people from all walks of life, seemed to have things in perspective. The items lost were material and replaceable; no human lives were taken and we were thankful.

Perhaps, it is in life's upsets, we are given the opportunity to grow, learning what we can

♥ SON Salutations

when tragedy strikes. Yet, there may also be times when our load seems too heavy to bear.

Thankfully, someone is there who we can call on in times of trouble or joy. His name is Jesus Christ, the Son of God, and it is only through Him that we have salvation.

Are you thankful for all you have...food, shelter, employment, and loved ones?
All these are important, but without Christ in your life, all the riches in the world will not offer you eternal life.

A Marriage In Christ

"There is nothing more lovely in life than the union of two people whose love for one another has grown through the years from a small acorn of passion to a great rooted tree. Surviving all vicissitudes, and rich with its manifold branches, every leaf holding its own significance." --Vita Sackville-West

In the Bible, we are told of the ultimate relationship between husband and wife; it is God's desire for husband and wife to no longer be two beings on separate paths, but be united as one flesh. (*"For this reason a man will leave his father and mother and be united to his wife, and the two will become one flesh." - Ephesians 5:31*) The word 'united' in this verse refers to being joined, as one, connected. The reason for this bonded state is quite simple and is explained in the following verse: *"He who loves his wife loves himself. After all, no one ever hated his own body, but he feeds and cares for it, just as Christ does the church - for we are members of his body."*
- Ephesians 5:28-29

We are also told husbands should love their wives in such a way that the female is built up and blessed by her husband's presence.

Think, for a moment, of the type of marital relationship that would result in a wife (bride) actually being edified by her husband (groom).

Logically, there would have to be complete trust, mutual respect, kindness, caring, and obviously, a genuine love. A wife, who regards her spouse in this manner, has no problem placing her very life in the arms of her husband, for he will love his bride as he loves his own body. While it is true these verses in Ephesians discuss the unique union of husband and wife, they, at the same time, are used to describe our relationship with Jesus Christ, who is often referred to in the Bible, as the "groom," with the body of Believer's or Church called the "bride."

Christ's love for us is so strong that nothing can separate us from him. Just as husband and wife are joined as one, those who place their trust, their very life, in Christ's hands are members of his body. As Christ's bride, (those who believe in him) place the Groom (Jesus Christ, the Son of God) at the head of the Church, we, too, must place Christ at the forefront of our lives.

"Never will I leave you; never will I forsake you."
- Hebrews 13:5

Endings

The decision to let go of the past and embrace the future can indeed be scary, for, in doing so, one must release what is comfortable. As my grandmother used to say, "Old habits often die hard." You see, endings are merely the promise of new beginnings! It is all in how one regards change; for the better, it is always good and change for the sake of necessary adjustments in one's life, such as in the case of a newly widowed wife getting used to a life without her spouse, is a journey uncharted.

God's word mentions endings, beginnings, and transformations. *"Do not conform any longer to the pattern of this world, but be transformed by the renewing of your mind. Then you will be able to test and approve what God's perfect will is - his good, pleasing and perfect will." - Romans 12:2*

'Renewing your mind' is a firm decision to change that which is unproductive, harmful, and displeasing to God to that which is good in His sight. It is turning one's back to evil and stepping forward into the light, God's light.

Whether you made a decision to let go of a food, drug, or alcohol addiction, involvement in pornography, or an immoral lifestyle, God is there to be your strength and guiding force.

Close the door to sin, but open another door to

♥ SON Salutations

His good and perfect ways.

"Therefore, if anyone is in Christ, he is a new creation; the old has gone, the new has come!" - II Corinthians 5:17

About The Author

Melanie Schurr is the author of the 2004 release, **Ecstatic Living/ Ecstatic Loving**: *A Christian marriage manual and life-guide.* The author, who has been married 20 yrs., presents an honest and detailed book on how to add more passion, meaning, and intimacy to marriage. Also covers dealing with teens, difficult relationships, healing from a painful past, having a healthy mind, body and spirit, the differences in the sexes, the power of prayer, and various other topics which affect daily life. Book is an excellent resource for couples in troubled marriages, or those which just need a shot in the arm! *Some portions may not be suitable for children.* Available at most major on-line book stores, LotusBooks.net or ask your local bookstore to order (no charge) ISBN 1-4116-2350-9.

Melanie Schurr is a multi-published free-lance writer who has contributed to both the secular and Christian media in newspaper, magazine & internet. The 44 year old wife and mother is a former newspaper columnist , and continues to be a 8+ year weekly contributing writer for "Daily Wisdom," (www. daily wisdom.com), which is sponsored by "The Gospel

♥ SON Salutations

Communications Network," (www.gospelcom.net). Schurr also is currently a writer for Spirit magazine (www.spirit-mag.com) and is founder of Lotus Books (LotusBooks.net) publishing services, an affordable publishing service with rates as low as $99.00 for writers/authors who desire to self publish.

Schurr's inspirations strive to lead the reader to a deeper relationship with God. It is not uncommon for *Daily Wisdom* readers to contact the author for informal advice and prayer, and for Church educators world-wide to seek reprint permission for use in sermons, Bible studies and newsletters.

The author has two children, one who is serving in our nation's Armed Forces. Visit the author at LotusBooks.net

Lotus Books Publishing Services

$10.00 off any service package

LOTUSBOOKS.NET
Clip this coupon and include with your publishing service payment

Contact: editor@LotusBooks.net

Expiration Date: January 1, 2006

A refreshing collection of daily inspirations ♥ *321*

♥ SON Salutations